NEW ZEALAND'S SECRET HEROES

NEW ZEALAND'S SECRET HEROES

Don Stott and the 'Z' Special Unit

GABRIELLE McDONALD

First published 1991 by Reed Books,
a division of Octopus Publishing Group (NZ) Ltd,
39 Rawene Road, Birkenhead, Auckland. Associated companies,
branches and representatives throughout the world.

Copyright © Gabrielle McDonald 1991

This book is copyright. Except for the purpose of fair reviewing, no part
of this publication may be reproduced or transmitted in any form or by
any means, electronic or mechanical, including photocopying, recording,
or any information storage and retrieval system, without permission in
writing from the publisher. Infringers of copyright render themselves
liable to prosecution.

ISBN 0 7900 0216 7

Printed in New Zealand

CONTENTS

Foreword by Brigadier Eddie Myers, CBE, DSO — *vii*
Preface — *ix*
Acknowledgments — *xi*
Glossary — *xiii*

Prologue — *xv*

PART ONE
Introduction — 3
1. Early Days in Greece — 5
2. The Asopos Viaduct — 21
3. Rendezvous with the Germans — 36
4. Preparation for Borneo — 46

PART TWO
Introduction — 57
5. Survive or Die — 58
6. Operation Jaywick — 67
7. The Tragedy that was Rimau — 77
8. The Formation of 'Z' Special Unit — 85
9. For Special Duties — 92
10. Encounter with the Japanese — 102
11. Living with the Headhunters of Borneo — 115
12. The Final Surrender — 130

Epilogue — 143
Appendices — 148
Bibliography — 164
Index — 166

DEDICATION

To the memory of

my grandfather, Sergeant William Bernard Ward, who fought for freedom with the 20th Battalion in the Western Desert, and lost his life at Minqar Qaim on 28 June 1942,

and also to the memory of

four young New Zealanders from 'Z' Special Unit, who gave more than their best, and died in service for their country far from their homeland:

Major Donald Stott, DSO & Bar	20 March 1945
WO2 Robert Houghton	26 March 1945
Captain Leslie McMillan	20 March 1945
Signalman Ernest Myers	30 June 1945

*'I loved you, so I drew these tides of men into my hands
and wrote my will across the sky in stars
To earn you Freedom, the seven pillared worthy house,
that your eyes might be shining for me
When we came.'*

T.E. LAWRENCE

FOREWORD
by Brigadier Eddie Myers, CBE, DSO

In this admirable, vividly written and largely factual story, the author pays tribute to some of the exploits of members of the Special Operations Executive (known as SOE) behind the enemy lines in Greece and the Far East, mainly Borneo.

The outstanding hero in this book is the late Major Don Stott, a New Zealander who earned his first DSO whilst under my command with the British Mission to the Resistance in enemy-occupied Greece; and his second one also in Greece during the time of my successor and previous second-in-command, Colonel the Hon. C. M. (Chris) Woodhouse. Stott was undoubtedly the bravest man we ever knew, and it is perfectly accurate for the author to state that had a shot been fired during the destruction of the Asopos Viaduct, vividly described here, Stott would probably have been awarded the VC for which I had recommended him.

It is a great privilege to have been invited to write the Foreword to this story because of my acquaintanceship, not only with Don, but with several other outstanding New Zealanders during the Second World War. Two of these were the late Tom Barnes, and the very-much-alive Arthur Edmonds, both Royal Engineer officers, who were among my original party of 12 who parachuted into the Greek mountains in the autumn of 1942 to cut Rommel's supply line through Greece. They both proved to be great sappers, cool in action, resourceful and utterly dependable. Another was the late Bill Jordan, who was especially dropped in to us a little later to sort out our wireless communications with SOE Cairo and to get them to work. Jordan was a great character with a low flash-point, and he achieved his task brilliantly.

The account of Stott's fantastic activities in and around Athens after the destruction of the Asopos Viaduct must be read bearing in mind that all our widely separated British Liaison Officers (BLOs) were only very loosely under my, or later Chris Woodhouse's, day-to-day control. Our portable, short-wave wireless sets were incapable of giving us communication with each other within Greece. All wireless messages between us had to be transmitted via Cairo. Written messages by runners over the mountains might take several days and were therefore of only limited use. With the best will in the world, and the most careful wording, delicate operational, let-alone political, situations were not always correctly interpreted by recipients.

During Don's dangerous contacts with the Germans, resulting from the local Gestapo's peace overtures to him, I have every reason to believe that Don kept SOE Cairo informed about most stages of his activities. But SOE Cairo failed to keep Chris Woodhouse informed, presumably because of their sensitivity.

After the end of the war in Europe, I was posted to Lord Mountbatten's headquarters in Ceylon, and later Singapore as head of counter-intelligence. Within a month of my arrival the war was over in the Far East. Although my immediate post-war duties took me for a few days to the Australian Army Headquarters in Morotai, and on a short visit to Balikpapan, I was never closely involved with SOE operations in the Far East. The operations in the jungles of enemy-occupied Borneo, so thrillingly described in Part Two of this book, called for different techniques from those required in enemy-occupied Greece. What was certainly required when operating under both conditions, however, was self-confidence.

The New Zealanders in SOE whom I was privileged to know, although not necessarily fearless, certainly had developed broad shoulders and an abundance of self-confidence. Most of them, I feel sure, had the advantage of having been brought up in rural, rather than urban surroundings. Since childhood they had learned to stand on their own feet, to do their duty and to fend for themselves. They were good soldiers. I salute them all.

Brigadier Eddie Myers, CBE, DSO

PREFACE

I count myself fortunate to have been born in an age without war. I have never known what it was like to live in a time when there were shortages — shortages of men, food, clothing, and all the essentials that we, a generation born after the Second World War, take so much for granted.

A father or a grandfather away from home, fighting a war on the other side of the world, and his loved ones at home, praying for his safe return. And when he does not return, the awful loneliness and heartbreak, and knowing that his voice will never be heard again.

I started out originally to write a book about New Zealand's unsung heroes of the Second World War, never dreaming that I would uncover a highly secret and unheard-of group of daring commandos — 'Z' Special Unit. These young men suffered unspeakable hardships and sufferings to do 'their duty' for their country. After hard, tough training at Commando School, they were prepared for any eventuality. That way they could not fail.

Few people have heard the name of Don Stott. I had never heard of him until three years ago, when I began my research on 'Z' Special Unit. His name occurred so frequently that I had a yearning to find out more about him, and also about his companion Bob Morton. The fact that he had died just before the war finished, leaving a young widow and son, was not in itself unusual. This so often happens in war — a young warrior who has finally come to the end of his nine lives. What was extraordinary was the feats of daring he achieved in such a short military career.

Other New Zealanders' names cropped up regularly as well, including Bill Horrocks and Frank Wigzell, who fought in the jungles, mountains and swamps of Japanese-occupied Borneo. Wigzell, according to Australian Fred Sanderson, 'was afraid of nothing'.

No one I spoke to in New Zealand had ever heard of 'Z' Special Unit, and the New Zealand Army was not forthcoming with any information either. It could not, or would not, help in any way. They had no knowledge, they said, of any operations, or any of the operatives who served with that unit.

By a series of unexplained coincidences and amazing luck I was able to piece together, little by little, the story of these remarkable men. Remember their ages, as you read this story — the oldest was 30 and the youngest 19.

I feel I am fortunate indeed to have been given the opportunity, and very proud, to write about these New Zealanders.

Gabrielle McDonald

ACKNOWLEDGMENTS

So many people have helped me in the preparation of this manuscript. I am indebted to them for their advice, support and encouragement during the three years it has taken me to write this book. I wish to thank particularly the Stott family — Mary Fox, Geoffrey Stott, Diane Fox, and Edna and Bill Meehan of Christchurch; Barbara and Alwyn Louis, John and Janet Stott, Bob Stott, Lorraine and Ron Mills, and Graham Stott, all of Auckland. Thanks especially to Barbara for her kindness and her help, and for permission to reprint from Don's diaries and papers; to Brigadier Myers in England, for his encouragement, reading my manuscript, offering suggestions, and for writing the Foreword to this book. Also in England to the Hon. C. M. (Chris) Woodhouse for his help and advice, and to Sir Peter Wilkinson.

In Greece to my uncle and aunt, Roger and Angela Ward, for their help and support; to Themie Marinos, the late Spiros Kotsis, and Nicholas Kyrtatos.

In Australia to Ronald McKie, Bill Dwyer, Horrie Young, and all the Australian members of 'Z' Special Unit. Special thanks to Lt Colonel 'Jumbo' Courtney for his advice and permission to quote from his manuscript on 'Z' Special Unit.

To King's College, Liddell Hart Centre in London, Richard Taylor and Kate O'Brien, for the reproduction of photos, and to Marie Wood from the Australian War Memorial in Canberra, for the photos of Operation Jaywick.

In New Zealand to Hilda Bennett (née Morton) and to Hope, goes my love and gratitude; to Bernard Bookman, Jackson Madill, Keith Roper, Ross Shakes, Trevor Blaker, Allen Forrester, Marika Begg, Dr Keith Simcock, Harry Cotterill, Alan Boyd, Jack and Molly Hinton, Joan Bogue, Kenny Little, Jim McDevitt, Bill Allison, the late Brigadier Jim Burrows, and Danny McLaughlin — my grateful thanks.

To the late Bill Horrocks, and to my dear friends Annette, Adrienne, Lynn and Dulcie, who gave me their support and love; to Derek, who somehow kept me going throughout, and to Basil, whose idea it was that I should write about the unsung heroes, and for his constant encouragement

Acknowledgments

and help, and to Ian Watt, my publisher — my thanks.

To Frank, without whose help this book would not have been written — my grateful thanks. And lastly, to all my family — my sister Sue, my mother, and my father, who found Bill Horrocks for me, and who told me about 'Z' Special Unit, and especially to Clive and the children, Paul, Laurence, Fleur and Luke, for your love and your faith in me, and who had to put up with a part-time mother for many months.

Thanks are due to the following for supplying photographs and maps for this book:

Brigadier E. C. W. Myers: pp. vii, 23; R. H. Stott: pp. 6, 7, 9, 12, 13, 47, 53; Liddell Hart Centre, King's College, London: pp. 14, 20, 24, 25, 27, 29, 33; The Hon. C. M. Woodhouse: p. 42; R. M. Morton: pp. 51, 62; The *Auckland Star*: p. 49; Ross Shakes: p. 70; The Australian War Memorial: pp. 71, 73, 81; Frank Wigzell: pp. 61, 63, 65, 66, 87, 89, 91, 93, 100, 105, 118, 120, 125, 127, 132, 133, 134, 139, 140, 141, 142, 145.

GLOSSARY

ADC	Aide-de-camp (An officer attendant on a General)
AIB	Allied Intelligence Bureau
AIF	Australian Imperial Force
Arak	Rice alcohol
ATIS	Allied Translation & Interpretation Service
ATS	Auxiliary Territorial Services
Auster	Light aircraft
BBCAU	British Borneo Civil Administration Unit
Betty	Japanese bomber
BIF	Borneo Interior Force
BMM	British Military Mission
Borak	Fermented drink made from rice or tapioca root
Boston	Wireless transceiver
Bukit	Hill
Chute	Parachute
CO	Commanding Officer
DCM	Distinguished Conduct Medal
DSO	Distinguished Service Order
DZ	Dropping Zone
EAM	National Liberation Front, Greece
EDES	National Republican Greek League
ELAS	National People's Liberation Army (Military Branch of EAM)
Eureka Rebecca	Ground-to-air signal beacon
F/L	Flight Lieutenant
Flight 200	Special Duties Flight RAAF
F/O	Flying Officer
Folboat	Native boat similar to an Eskimo kayak
Fujino Tai	Japanese force under Captain Fujino
GHQ	General Headquarters
HQ	Headquarters
Jaywick	SRD party's raid on Singapore
Kampong	Village

Glossary

Kempei Tai	Japanese Secret Police
Kepala	Head
Kiai	Teacher (religious or scholar)
Kuala	river mouth or estuary
LMG	Light machine-gun
MC	Military Cross
MM	Military Medal
MSC	Motor submersible canoe
NCOs	Non-commissioned Officers
Orang Puteh	White man
Padang	Village green
Parang	Native sword
Penghulu	Headman of small district
Perahu	Native dugout canoe
POW	Prisoner-of-war
RAAF	Royal Australian Air Force
RAP	Regimental Aid Post
Rimau	SRD's repeat, or second raid, on Singapore Harbour
Robin 1	'Z' Special Unit's reconnaissance party into Balikpapan
Robin 2	'Z' Special Unit's party into Balikpapan to find members of Robin 1
Round House	Railway depot
Rumah	House
Sapper	Engineer
SEAC	South-East Asia Command
Semut	Ant
Sked	Wireless transmission
SMG	Sub-machine-gun
SOA	Special Operations Australia
SOE	Special Operations Executive (London)
SO	Special Operations
SRD	Services Reconnaissance Department
Storepedos	Cylindrical containers for dropping stores
Sulap	Small hut or shelter
Sumpitan	Blowpipe
Tuan	White chief
Ulu	Interior
Wellrod	Silent single-shot pistol
WO2	Warrant Officer Second Class
W/T	Wireless telegraphy

PROLOGUE

20 March 1945

On a dark stormy night in the closing months of the Second World War an American submarine, the USS *Perch*, surfaced in a thick swell 56 km from Balikpapan, off the coast of enemy-occupied Borneo. On board the submarine were 12 commandos from Z Special Unit, a specially trained group of secret agents and saboteurs. Five were New Zealanders, three were Australians, while another three were from the Dutch East Indies. They were accompanied by one Malay interpreter.

The men's faces were blackened, and they wore jungle greens with camouflaged floppy hats and green canvas, lace-up commando boots. On each man's back was webbing gear containing magazines and ammunition, a small pack with extra ammunition, together with enough emergency food and material supplies to last for a few days in the jungle. They carried torches, a compass, trade money and, just above the boot, a 20 cm stiletto knife, the deadly trade mark of the para-commando. The men had the choice of either a sub-machine-gun or a US .30 calibre Carbine, and a Smith & Wesson revolver or a US .45 calibre Colt automatic pistol.

Sergeant Bill Horrocks, from Auckland, New Zealand, was taut and nervous. This was his first operation. Beads of perspiration dotted his forehead like wisps of dew, and his legs felt as if they didn't belong to him. There was a lump in the pit of his stomach and his mouth was dry. There was no turning back.

The *Perch* drifted slowly into Balikpapan Bay and stopped about 1 100 metres from the foreshore. Only 4 of the 12 commandos on board the submarine were to go into the Japanese-occupied Balikpapan Bay area. The other eight, under the command of New Zealander Captain Bob Morton, were to rendezvous with the four men approximately two days later.

The four operatives quietly assembled their folboats (similar to kayaks) on the deck of the submarine at 2200 hours. In a matter of minutes everything was ready. The men shook hands with the rest of the operatives.

New Zealander Major Don Stott, DSO & Bar, the leader of the party, farewelled his partner and great friend, Captain Morton. The two old friends hugged each other, not knowing if they would see one another again. There had been so much to say before, and now, suddenly, there was nothing left to say.

'Are you ready, boys?' asked the Commander of the *Perch*, Blish Hills. 'Good luck, and safe return!'

By now the weather was starting to deteriorate rapidly. Thunder crashed and lightning crackled across the black sky and heavy rain started to pelt the men in their light clothing. Horrocks felt for his cyanide capsule sewn into the lapel of his shirt.

The two folboats were pushed over the side. The men lowered themselves into these, and hung on grimly to the sides as the waves crashed about them. Horrocks wanted to scramble back on to the submarine, but it was too late. It had started to submerge.

Aucklanders Stott and Captain Leslie McMillan were in Folboat No. 1. Sergeants Horrocks and Bruce Dooland, an Australian cricketer, were in the second folboat. Each man had a high-frequency walkie-talkie, which they were to use in the event of their being separated.

McMillan sat in the front, and Stott in the back. Stott went to start the outboard motor. Nothing happened, so he tried again. Still nothing happened. By now a gale was in full force, the waves breaking all around them and swamping them in their light rubber craft. Stott shouted to McMillan over the noise of the wind and rain to use the paddles.

They could see Horrocks and Dooland just ahead of them, desperately trying to make for the shore. Suddenly, in between flashes of lightning Stott, to his horror, saw lights dotted along the shore area.

He yelled to McMillan: 'Christ! There's bloody Nips on the shore! We're sitting ducks!'

Sweat poured down Stott's face and, together with the rain, stung his eyes. What to do now? He knew he had no choice. They could not return to the submarine. He gave the last order of his life.

Horrocks' walkie-talkie crackled into action.

'Enemy in sight!' said Stott's voice. 'Go for your lives!'

The men struck out in different directions. Two of them landed on the soils of Borneo for the first time.

Don Stott was never seen again.

PART 1

INTRODUCTION

On 6 April 1941 Greece was invaded by German troops which had also invaded Yugoslavia and Bulgaria. A British force of over 60 000 men, including the Second New Zealand Division and the 6th Australian Division, quickly went to the aid of the Greek Army. The gallant but unequal campaigns of Greece in April and Crete in May shook the morale of the British Army and also of the Greek people.

A considerable number of allied soldiers were left on the mainlands of Greece and Crete because of the lack of ships to uplift them. Some escaped capture by hiding in the hills, while others later joined the Resistance as part of the Special Operations Executive, known through this book as SOE.

SOE in Cairo decided to send the Hon. C. M. (Chris) Woodhouse, an Oxford classical scholar, to Crete to contact Australians and New Zealanders who had been unable to be evacuated. Woodhouse returned to Cairo five months later, and in the summer of 1942 Brigadier E. C. W. (Eddie) Myers of the British Army, together with Colonel Woodhouse as his second-in-command, were sent into Greece to start a British Military Mission.

They were also to command an operation to destroy one of the principal railway bridges in the mountains, thereby disrupting German troops, and so delaying reinforcements being sent to the Western Desert.

A party of 12 men from SOE, including Tom Barnes and Arthur Edmonds from New Zealand, successfully blew up the Gorgopotamos railway viaduct in the mountains of Roumeli in November 1942. This was the only operation in Greece during the war in which the forces of ELAS — a Communist guerilla force under the leadership of Ares Veloukhiotis, and EDES, led by Napoleon Zervas, co-operated successfully.

However, the British Military Mission was to become entangled in a political, as well as a military war in Greece. As Myers himself wrote in his *Greek Entanglement*: 'British officers had to hurry hither and thither, keeping the peace; sometimes, as they did so, suffering rebuke, and even insults, from the political advisers of ELAS. For high-spirited officers, who had volunteered for hazardous sabotage work, the tasks which I had given to many of them called for the greatest efforts in patience and tact.'

This, then, was the world in which a young New Zealand officer, Donald Stott from Auckland, found himself when he parachuted into Greece in the spring of 1943 as part of Myers' British Military Mission.

CHAPTER 1

Early Days in Greece

'. . . I could be very happy here with even a third of my former estate if those friends of mine were still alive who died long ago on the broad plains of Troy so far from Argos where the horses graze.'

HOMER, *THE ODYSSEY*

Donald John Stott was born on 23 October 1914 in Birkenhead, Auckland, the youngest child and fourth son of Robert and Annie Stott. He attended Northcote District School and Takapuna Grammar, where he excelled in athletics, particularly the high jump, a sport which was to be a great help to him in Greece later on.

All the Stotts were red-haired, slender and tall, with even the only daughter, Ethel, almost 1.82 m tall.

The Stotts were a hard-working family, and instilled a stronge sense of values into their youngsters. They emphasised hard work, determination, and making the best of life. With his three brothers and sister, Don took his turn helping his father's butchery business in Birkenhead, which continues to this day.

His parents were Brethren but although Don was brought up strictly the family was a close and happy one. Annie Stott was close to all her children. Don's brother Bob says today from his home in Birkenhead: 'We could go to Mum with any problem at all. She was the most wonderful person really. I don't think I ever heard Mum say an unkind word against anybody. We all loved her dearly.'

Don was a happy, outgoing boy, who had his fair share of getting into mischief but even at a young age he was starting to display that determination and sense of fair play for which he would be renowned many

Robert and Annie Stott with their children (left to right): Ethel, Alexander, Hector, Robert and Donald.

years later. He was a late maturer with a strong love for animals.

When he left school he joined the staff of the *New Zealand Herald* in Auckland as a rotary machinist. He was with the *Herald* in 1939 when war broke out. He enlisted with the Second New Zealand Expeditionary Force in 1940, and quickly rose to the rank of Sergeant in the Artillery. Stott had had no military experience before he enlisted but his maternal grandfather and two of his uncles were regular soldiers in the Royal Scots Regiment.

The 26-year-old Stott made friends easily in the Army, and his tall athletic figure could always be seen either on the rugby field or in whatever athletic game was in progress at camp.

During 1940 he left New Zealand with the Second Echelon as an Artillery Sergeant. He fought in Greece and the Crete campaign of May 1941, where he was wounded and captured by German paratroopers. An x-ray later showed there was a shattered bullet behind his right knee joint. Stott spent two months in a POW camp on the outskirts of Athens where he met up with another New Zealander, Bob Morton.

Stott and Morton were vastly dissimilar types. Ruggedly handsome, Robert McDonald Morton was from Dargaville, north of Auckland, and

Don Stott and Bob Morton.

was as dark as Stott was fair. In the POW camp at Kokinia, a former Turkish army barracks, they formed a close friendship, and joined the camp athletic group. The one thought in their minds was of escape and what better way to do it than by pole vaulting? They practised every day, and when they had reached the required height to vault the prison wire, an escape committee set the day for the attempt.

At the camp athletic meeting, several POWs sat near the fence and watched as the guards relaxed and enjoyed their games.

When it came to the high vault, the guards couldn't believe what they saw. Stott and Morton, instead of running at the jump area, headed for the fence, vaulted over the obstacle perimeter wire, landed safely on the other side, and headed for the cover of the thick bush nearby.

The German guards were so amazed that for a few moments they did not fire any shots. By the time they had recovered, Stott and Morton had a head start. As they raced through the cover, zig-zagging to avoid the shots, Greek police who had seen the escape fired their pistols into the air.

The Greeks pointed a direction for Stott and Morton to head for, and they themselves rushed off in another direction, still firing their weapons. This fooled the Germans into following them in the wrong direction.

This was one of the most daring escapes that took place from a POW camp, and one of the first daylight escapes made by Allied POWs in Greece.

Another New Zealander, Jack Hinton, who was to be later awarded the Victoria Cross for gallantry in Kalamata, Greece, reminisces: 'I remember that day so well. The perimeter wire around the barracks was 6 feet [1.82 m] or more, and we [the prisoners] were amazed and relieved to see Stott clear it.'

In a letter home months later, Stott wrote to his mother: '. . . while I was convalescing in hospital from my wounds on Crete, I met up with Jim [Rowe]. He and I talked about escaping, and when we were transferred to the same camp I told Jim he must come with Bob and me. But Jim thought he would be a liability, and encouraged us to go without him. I hated leaving him. The last thing I remember hearing as I jumped that fence was old Jim shouting out "Go for it! Good luck!"'

Stott and Morton raced for the hills, but were lost for two days and nights, and very nearly died of thirst. Finally two Greek woodsmen found them and gave them water. After they had spent a further three days in the hills, their Greek friends managed to smuggle old clothes to them before they finally made their way back to Athens. For the next seven months they were on the run, wandering in the mountains around Athens, and on several occasions hiding in the city itself.

During these months they were continually hungry. The city of Athens was desperately short of food, and people were starving. There were survival rations only.

They spent some months in the south coast area, making many friends amongst the Greeks, and learning the language to the best of their ability.

During their stay on the south coast, they were forced to live on octopus, snails and seaweed, as food was almost impossible to buy or procure.

In a letter home to his mother, Stott mentions that food in Athens at that time was extremely expensive, with meat at 15/- a pound, and one egg 2/6d. (Back in New Zealand butter was 1/5d per pound, cheese was 1/- per pound, eggs 1/6d per dozen and sausages 1/- per pound.) Shortly before they left Athens Stott and Morton heard that 400 Greeks had died of starvation in a single day.

Eventually, some Greeks gave them a small sailboat in which they made two unsuccessful attempts to cross the Aegean Sea to Turkey, but were forced back by bad weather. On the third attempt they managed to cross the Mediterranean Sea and reached their base camp at Alexandria in Egypt. The pair were sent on recuperative leave.

Stott was, of course, under oath to say nothing in his letters home about what had really happened but he told his mother and father he had had experiences 'that would do justice to a fiction magazine . . . we had two narrow squeaks from the Gestapo and also the Caribineri'.

One of these incidents occurred when Stott and Morton, disguised as Greeks, were sitting in an Athens cinema watching a German propaganda news film. At one point Stott laughed derisively at an absurd news item, and during the interval they noticed two German officers eyeing them very closely. When the lights went out after the interval Stott and Morton made their escape quickly.

Another time Stott, again disguised as a Greek, was serving drinks in a

Stott disguised as a Greek for life as a saboteur with the underground.

German Officers' Club in Athens. (There was always the chance that he would overhear conversations which could be of military significance, and which he would be able to pass on.) One evening, to his horror, Gestapo officers walked in. They looked oddly at Stott and asked him one or two questions. Stott mumbled something in Greek, and then escaped out the back door as quickly as possible.

One day in May 1942, Stott was sitting in class at Officers' Training School in the Middle East when he was asked to report to General Headquarters. He was taken before the Naval Commissioner, who asked if he would be interested in going back to Greece for sabotage work. After his experiences, he might have been expected to settle down to an ordinary life as a soldier but by this time he was suffering from 'cloak and dagger disease'.

Stott was overjoyed, and said he would do anything at all, but there was just one condition: Gunner Bob Morton must be taken as well. The Commissioner thought it an excellent idea to keep the men together, but unfortunately at that time Morton was in the guardhouse!

Bernard Bookman, who was with the 5th New Zealand Field Regiment at this time, knew both Stott and Morton well.

'When Stott and Morton finally made it back to Egypt' he says, 'we were resting, between actions, near Bagush on the Egyptian coast. Don was sent off to Officer Cadet Training Unit (OCTU) and Morton came back to his unit, 27 Battery 5th Field. After such a long absence Bob was surprised and delighted at the unaccustomed credit balance in his pay book. He was always full of humour and loved a good time, so he quickly arranged to buy up the NAAFI [Naval, Army and AirForce Institute] supply of beer and turned on a memorable party for all his friends.

'In the high jinks that followed, Bob had insufficient time to sober up for the pre-dawn roll call "check parade". Some of his mates had not been able to wake up for this, so Bob decided to answer for them. The Sergeant on duty realised immediately what was happening and questioned Morton. Morton was still under the influence and decided to take matters into his own hands. With one well-placed punch, he laid the Sergeant out cold. Needless to say, he was duly charged and sentenced to 14 days' field punishment in the dreaded Citadel, at Abbassia near Cairo.

'The Citadel was run by the British Army, which had a completely different system from our own. The Citadel had the reputation for the most severe punishment. It was out to break the men sent there, and anyone who was in that unfortunate position knew they were in for the harshest treatment.

'However, before Bob's sentence was up, we were astonished — incredulous in fact — to see him back in our lines, grinning from ear to ear, and immaculate in brand-new battledress with, of all things, three stripes on his sleeve and the rank of full sergeant. He had the most remarkable story.

'At OCTU, Officer Cadet Don Stott had been approached to undertake "special duties" which he accepted on the condition that Bob Morton could join him. Stott was immediately commissioned, and Morton was yanked out of the guardhouse, dusted off, rekitted, promoted to Sergeant on the spot, and optimistically placed on some sort of good behaviour bond.'

Stott had had to wait two weeks before Morton was released, and during that time he was given 50 pounds to buy clothes. Although he was commissioned, he still wore cadet clothes. He walked into the officers' shop where he bought two pips and an officer's cap, much to the surprise of the British ATS girl behind the counter. He pinned on his pips, put his new cap on his head, and walked out an officer! As he came out of the shop, he met Regimental Sergeant-Major Rowlan of the Scots Guards, who threw him the best salute he had ever seen in his life.

Morton and Stott were told to report not to Greece, as they had hoped, but to Bardia, in Egypt. As Bardia is close to Crete, this was almost as good as Greece, and the excited pair boarded an old Italian truck for the trip.

They duly arrived in Bardia where there was a settlement of various naval and military people. They joined a Royal Naval group which ran a ferry service between Bardia and Crete, transporting POWs. After a time Stott started to get itchy feet, and applied for a transfer back to Greece. He felt he owed it to the Greek people who had helped him to escape from Greece to return and do all he could to free their country.

It was now July 1942, and the war in the Middle East had taken a turn for the worse, with the British being pushed back to the Alamein Line, a narrow but strategically important piece of ground approximately 160 km west of Alexandria and about 65 km in length. Stott and Morton arrived back in Alexandria, and then went to Palestine for a special course in demolition and sabotage.

Back in Cairo, Stott was posted to the Post Occupational Force. The men in this force were allocated definite contracts. Morton joined Stott and their

Stott and Morton in Cairo.

orders were to destroy the Maconi road works and installations at Abu Zabal. They were the only people who knew that arrangements had been made to destroy important installations in the town. Stott's name was changed to Andonius Stavros. Stott notes in his diary at this time that he found the situation he was in as humorous, as 'the whole situation in Cairo was treated in typical English style with people running around with false moustaches, hats, and so on . . .'

The Egyptian Army itself, however, was anti-British in its outlook, and at Abu Zabal, where Stott and Morton were stationed for three months, a battalion of Egyptian infantry guarded the place with orders that it was not to be destroyed by either the British or the Germans. Stott knew that this meant that the Egyptians would give way to the Germans rather than the British.

When the Alamein Line was seen to be holding, Stott and Morton withdrew from Abu Zabal, and applied once more for a transfer to Greece. While they were waiting for an answer, they were allotted a car and a flat in Cairo, and initially 50 pounds. Their main object was to remain above suspicion. About this time, a letter arrived in New Zealand and it found its way to Mrs Stott. It contained the news that one young soldier had seen Stott in Cairo. 'Do you know what?' it said. 'I saw Don Stott the other day, walking around Cairo as large as life, but wearing civilian clothes, of all things . . .'

Shortly after this, a report was sent to security asking who Stott and Morton were, and consequently they were quickly withdrawn from the field of action. By this time, Stott was getting fed up, and he quickly let it

Stott in Cairo with the car given to him by SOE Cairo.

be known that he was disappointed with the course of events so far. The man he saw was Colonel John Stevens, Liaison Officer for SOE (Cairo). Stott explained again that he had left field artillery to do one specific job, and that was to go back to Greece. He had been given jobs which were further away than ever from Greece.

'Is it worth while carrying on?' he asked Stevens.

Stevens told Stott he was going to take charge of the Greek Section shortly. 'If you stick around, I'll see you right. We need your type,' he said.

Stevens duly took charge of the Greek Section, and shortly afterwards, Stott, Morton and another New Zealander, Bill Jordan, began parachute training, with a view to parachuting into occupied Greece. Up until then no one had been dropped into Greece by parachute.

In the middle of August 1942, the three men began training in earnest at the Middle East Parachutist Training School at Kabrit, near Port Said, and beside the Suez Canal. Stott remarks in his diary:

> At the parachute school, the methods were rather crude, and the training severe. During PT I strained my back rather badly. On one jump I did a bad landing, crashed and injured my back again quite badly. This left me with a bad twist. However, I was determined to say nothing, because I wanted to complete the course and get my wings. I jumped for the rest of the time with acute pain.

In a letter home, he remarked that he thought parachute training was the toughest and the most thorough training in the world. '. . . Bob is with me

— poor old Bob. I make the bullets and he's always dragged in to help fire them. It's doing us both the world of good, and anyway, we'll be pioneers in a way, as we are the first Kiwi parachutists.'

When the course was completed, Stott, Morton, and William Jordan were the first three New Zealanders to complete an organised parachute course. Jordan, who was to go on to become a Catholic priest after the war, wrote about his years with the Resistance in Greece in his book *Conquest Without Victory*.

Bill Jordan, who undertook parachute training with Stott and Morton.

At this time the Middle East Command was planning to break out of the El Alamein line. It was important to hinder the enemy in every way possible in their efforts to bring supplies by sea from southern Europe to their bases along the North African coast. One of the major routes was from Piraeus, the port of Athens, via Crete. Piraeus was served by a single-line standard-gauge railway, which served the coast of Salonica, southwards across the plains of Thessaly and through the steep mountains of Roumeli and Attitica, down to Athens and the coast. In Roumeli there were three large railway viaducts situated on the north-eastern edge of the mountain group of Giona. It was vital therefore that one or all of these viaducts be demolished, which would cut off the railway line for weeks, maybe months. These were the Gorgopotamos, the Asopos and the Papadia viaducts.

Whilst the three New Zealanders were completing their parachute training, a sabotage party, including two New Zealanders from General Headquarters, Middle East, blew up the Gorgopotamos Viaduct on 25 November 1942. The Gorgopotamos mission was organised and led by

Brigadier Eddie Myers, and for a time this severed Rommel's lifeline of supplies to Africa. Stott and Morton were annoyed that they had not been included in this sabotage expedition. In his diary Stott wrote: 'It is typical of GHQ that they overlooked the people who were more or less on the spot, and searched elsewhere for saboteurs. Morton and I had the local knowledge, good contacts, and a very good smattering of the language.'

Stott, Morton and Jordan, having completed the parachutist course, returned to Cairo to persuade headquarters to consent to their returning to Greece. Shortly after, Stott was made second-in-command of a party which was to go into Greece and start a British Mission to organise resistance and contact the guerilla element. A few days later, word came through to say that the whole operation was cancelled, as the Germans had captured the men who were working in the particular area where Stott was to be dropped. Had he parachuted in at that time he would have landed straight into German hands.

A couple of months later, Stott issued an ultimatum to Colonel Stevens: 'I'm fed up with the whole show,' he said. 'It looks as though I am being purposely kept out. Other chaps have been sent to Greece who came into the Section after Bob and I. I just don't consider we have been fairly treated.'

Stevens looked at the lanky New Zealander. Maybe a little over-enthusiastic, he thought. On the other hand, the man certainly had guts and determination.

'Look, we are sending a man next month,' he told Stott. 'A Major Gordon-Creed — you can go with him. We know you're very keen, and you have to go, but we were worried that if we had sent you before now you would have rushed straight to Athens, and got yourself caught and shot.'

Stott promised that he would be careful, and then was told that he was to be dropped into Greece with a wireless operator, who was to guide him to a British officer who had been dropped about a month earlier. Morton and Stott reported to the Special Air Service in Kabrit, where they saw a Major Rountree who briefed them on their operation.

Stott reported in his journal the following conversation: 'Your operation is going to take place on the 23 October (this was the 20th) and it is a highly hazardous one,' said Rountree. 'Stott, you are in complete command. This is where you will be dropped.'

Rountree pulled out a map and pointed right to the centre of the German lines on the Alamein front. 'Your job is to cut communications,' said Rountree. 'It may surprise you to know that a big offensive is going to take place on the night of the 23rd. This mission is entirely voluntary. It is a most important assignment. Rommel is in there. You know you can refuse to do this job. How many men do you want?'

'I only want one,' said Stott. 'Morton.'

Rountree told Stott he could not guarantee a safe passage out. 'I can't promise anything,' he said. 'You could walk to the coast where, we hope, but can't promise, you will be picked up by the Navy. Then again, you will probably run into trouble, as there is a strong force down the coast. The other method is to take a shovel, dig a hole, and sit in it until rescued!'

Understandably, Stott was unhappy with this situation. He was quite certain he was never coming out, and it seemed to be ironic that the day he was to leave should be his birthday.

On the morning of 23 October 1942, his 28th birthday, Stott and Morton left Kabrit in a Wellington bomber for Ambria and the 8th Army Headquarters. Stott was tired as he had not had any real sleep for days but he was determined to see the job through to its conclusion. At Ambria the men were given a last briefing and shown the latest air photographs, which were three days old. Stott had wanted more up-to-date photos, but had to be content with what he had been given.

He was taken to see the Commanding Officer, a Colonel Bill Sterling, holder of a Victoria Cross. Sterling shook his hand and wished him luck. Some American officers were there to see them off. Their fame had spread! Stott notes in his diary 'The Yanks were there to look over the bodies as it were! One of them said to me: "Say boy, we think you're mighty brave going on a suicide mission like this!"'

By this time, Stott was completely resigned to his fate, and strangely enough was worried less about it. It was a bright moonlit night and he was praying for cloud cover, as he knew that the Germans would see them, even though the aircraft and parachutes were camouflaged.

> 'It was amazing,' he writes. 'We were flying low, about 10 feet off the ground, so low that I was amazed to see the face of an Italian quite clearly leaning against his truck, and to see the surprise on his face. That will tell you how light it was. Guns were firing all around us, and there was flak everywhere. I said to myself, "We must get it any moment".'

The aircraft was now riddled with bullets, and it started to climb to 140 m. Just before the red light came on, a terrific explosion rocked the aircraft, and Stott was struck blind for some seconds. When he regained his sight and hearing, he saw Morton on the opposite of the parachute hole, covered with blood. He yelled to him through the noise: 'Don't go!'

Suddenly he saw the flash of the green light to go. He automatically moved over the hole to drop out of the aircraft, and was slipping out when he felt a hand grasp his collar and pull him back. It was the despatcher, Sergeant Markwell.

'I can well remember looking down as the green light came on and feeling myself going,' writes Stott. 'I could see the men below, shooting at us with guns and rifles. This was the area in which there were supposed to be no troops!'

They were told to report back to headquarters as fast as possible. It took two hours to reach Kabrit. There was a gigantic hole in the side of the aircraft and 200 bullet holes.

Stott was lucky to have escaped injury, but Morton was wounded in 17 places, and was extremely lucky to be alive. One bullet which might have gone completely through his lungs had pierced his automatic. One had hit his water bottle over his heart. Another bullet had taken his collar clean off, and his play line had been cut in half.

Before they had climbed into the aircraft, Stott had made Morton strap his water bottle and his automatic onto his chest to keep them clear of his parachute harness. Morton had not seen the point in doing this, and had had to be coerced. That action, of course, had saved his life.

In hospital Morton was visited by Bernard Bookman. Bookman had heard Stott and Morton had run into trouble on one of their hair-raising operations. He found out where Morton was and found him in a hospital bed, swathed in bandages from eyebrows to toenails. Morton told Bookman how lucky he had been.

'Stott is very thorough,' Morton said to Bookman. 'We had flown over for reconnaissance, sorted out where we wanted to drop and how we would get back, and had everything organised. Then, on the night, back we went and were all set to jump when, would you believe, we saw there was a bloody panzer division right in our jump area. I was relieved that we would be off the hook and told Don to get the hell out of there, but he said, "No, we're going to jump".

'I was scared stiff, and then the searchlights picked us up and we were being shot at. Then, fortunately for us, we were hit by ack-ack [anti-aircraft fire] and a shell exploded inside the plane. I was peppered with 20 or 30 bits of shrapnel, and we had to turn back so they could try to fish the pieces out of me.'

Bookman remarks that Bob Morton was one of those men who do unusually bold and brave things but don't hesitate to tell you how scared they are.

Morton was also remarkable in that he would have followed Stott out of the plane, despite his injuries.

At 8th Army headquarters, Stott reported on what he had seen in the area, but it was not until 3 a.m. that he was told that the whole mission had been abandoned. He breathed a sigh of relief, then went to bed and slept for three days.

Stott was now promised another operation to waylay Rommel, and was told to take two weeks' holiday. When he returned from holiday in Cyprus, he was put on a small reconnaissance of the Dodecanese Islands. Some of these islands were believed to be unoccupied, and could be useful in the future for any operation. He reconnoitred two small islands and then flew back to Cairo, where he found to his dismay that the other operation, the waylaying of Rommel, had already gone ahead. It was almost too much.

However, he should have been relieved — the men on that operation were never heard of again.

Finally, on 21 March 1943, and after many false starts, Stott, in the company of Major Geoffrey Gordon-Creed, was given his long-awaited chance, and set off on a mission to Greece. Geoffrey Gordon-Creed was a Rhodesian by birth, who had also joined 'the firm', as SOE was affectionately termed by its agents.

Both men wore ordinary battle-dress, with badges of rank under their parachuting kit. The kit consisted of a rubber helmet, a padded boiler suit (like Churchill's pyjama suit) and rubber-soled jumping boots. Underneath they each had a belt of gold sovereigns which was heavy and uncomfortable.

Their equipment was a mixture of the practical and the bizarre. They were armed with a .45 revolver and ammunition, a commando knife, a field-dressing (in case the knife slipped), a compass disguised as a button, a map disguised as a silk scarf, a mess-tin, a water-bottle, a tin of hard rations, a torch, two or three coloured flares, some benzedrine pills, a cyanide capsule, and a strong pair of leather-soled boots covered with metal studs.

The rest of their kit was packed in long metal cylinders along with explosives, hand-grenades, sten-guns, batteries and so forth. Their wirelesses and charging engines were attached to their parachutes, and the SOE operatives who dropped into Greece had to take special care that the radios did not drop on their heads when they landed.

Both Gordon-Creed and Stott were to join the British Military Mission run by Brigadier Myers in the Greek mountains. (Stott was also sent into Greece to sabotage bauxite-mine construction.) They flew for about four hours before they were over Greece, and the pilot began to search for the promised signal flares. Stott was both excited and sick with anticipation.

Gordon-Creed was white-faced as he climbed into his parachute harness in readiness for the jump.

'My God, you are looking sick,' he said to Stott.

'Not as sick as you're looking,' replied Stott.

For the next three-quarters of an hour they flew around the beautiful but cold Greek mountains, looking in vain for the landing flares. But there were none to be seen.

Suddenly the wireless operator shouted to them: 'Climb into your chute. We have sighed the signal flares!'

Stott yelled to Gordon-Creed to get ready, but there was no answer. He was being sick! The green light to go flashed on, and Stott jumped. This was his first operational jump. 'My God,' he thought to himself. 'What if I hit the ground before the 'chute opens! It should have opened by now. Oh, no, it's not going to open!'

And then, magically, he felt it tighten, and the parachute fluttered open like an umbrella. He looked over his shoulder, and saw the wireless operator far out to his left. He judged his height at about 1700 m. Too high! He was drifting miles away from the area he was supposed to drop in. But he was in Greece! Suddenly nothing mattered anymore. He was back in the country he loved, and soon he would be amongst the people who had run so many risks for him before. He could see the stars overhead, gradually disappearing into dark, black clouds.

He realised he was going to land in the worst part of the mountains. He was drifting too far away from the signal fires. Suddenly, without warning, a mountain came up towards him. He found himself crashing through some trees into the snow.

Although scratched and bruised, he felt elated. He released himself from the parachute harness, and left the parachute in the trees. The mountain was dotted with fir trees, and there was a smell of fresh pinewood all round him.

In the distance he could hear the throb of the engines of the aircraft which he had so recently left. There was no other sound to be heard, and the stillness and peacefulness around him indicated that he was completely alone.

Gordon-Creed had been dropped in another area of the mountains. Now Stott had to find his wireless operator, and was just about to blow his whistle in the hope that the wireless operator would hear it. However, he was reluctant to do this in case there were Germans about. Then he remembered he had seen a village nestled in the mountains, just before he landed, so he set out to find it. He had gone only a little way when he heard someone calling out. He answered in Greek and there was an immediate reply. They

Greek women helping with supplies dropped by parachute.

were friends! He was safe. The next moment several Greek guerillas came running up to him, kissing him on both cheeks. He kissed them right back, and everybody started talking excitedly.

The Greek guerillas took Stott to the village, where bottles of the Greek spirit, ouzo, were brought out. Stott told them about his parachute stuck in the tree back on the mountain, and also about the lost wireless operator who, by this time, must be looking everywhere for him.

The Greeks sent out a search party, and soon the wireless operator was brought in. He was a mountain of a man from Manchester County with a delightful sense of humour. His name was Dick Jones, and he couldn't speak a word of Greek. Consequently, he could understand nothing of what was going on around him. The pent-up emotions of the last few hours finally took over, and Stott and Jones fell into an exhausted sleep.

CHAPTER 2

The Asopos Viaduct

'It is a sad commentary on human values that war, which has accustomed us to death, should have brought with it so full and rich a sense of life.'

JOHN MULGAN, *REPORT ON EXPERIENCE*

The next day Stott reported to the local guerilla headquarters, and gave them as much information as he could. The nearest British officer was a day's march away, so after a good night's rest Stott, Jones, and a guide, Captain Costa (known by his first name, Kokovista) set off. The trails were narrow and precipitous, and although there were mules, the men decided to walk. Dick Jones weighed about 80 kg, and none of the mules was big enough for him anyway.

Nicholas Kyrtatos, Stott's interpreter while he was in Greece, recalls that Stott would ride side-saddle on a donkey because he was so tall that his long legs would touch the ground. They would burst into peals of laughter each time this happened. 'Sometimes I can't believe he's not alive,' says Kyrtatos. 'We faced so many dangers together and always came through.'

When they arrived at their destination, they met a British officer, Captain Nat Barker, who had parachuted in with Brigadier Myers' original party to Greece. They immediately radioed to Cairo to let them know they had arrived safely.

Three days later, Brigadier Myers — a quiet, reliable man in his thirties — arrived from northern Thessaly. 'With his maquisard's beard, high forehead and long, ascetic face, Myers looked like a saint in a Byzantine icon,' remarks André Kedros in his book *La Résistance Grecque*. Stott now had his first taste of how things were done in occupied Greece.

Stott told Myers that he had been sent to Greece to sabotage bauxite-mine construction. He reported their subsequent conversation in his diary:

> 'There is a lot of bauxite from Greece used in the manufacture of aluminium. I want to stop all construction,' I said.
>
> 'We don't work under these methods here,' said Myers. 'We allot an area to an officer, called a Liaison Officer, who is a member of the British Military Mission. He sees to sabotage in any area. He is politically, militarily, and financially responsible for that particular area. You look a good chap, and we need a liaison officer in the Parnassus area. I want you to go and try and contact Colonel Demetrios Psaros, Commander of the 5/42 Regiment (EKKA). I will promote you here and now to local Captain.'

Stott was thrilled, and pinned on his three pips.

It was at this time, approximately 28 March 1943, that Stott met Captain Themi Marinos, a young Greek who was one of the first members of the British Military Mission. Marinos was Brigadier Myers' ADC and interpreter.

'When I met Stott,' says Marinos, 'Myers released me from my duties as interpreter and entrusted me with the task of briefing Stott and guiding him to the area where Colonel Psaros was.'

Greece is a country well suited to guerilla warfare. Most of the country is mountainous, and the land is hard and barren. The few plains that exist are cut off by ranges of desolate hills. During the war, the roads were few and primitive, and the only communication in the mountain areas was by foot or mule. The Greek people, however, are hard-working, and spirited, and would never bow to any conqueror. Consequently, the Italians and the Germans were hated by the Greeks, who fought fiercely for their freedom.

Small bands of guerillas, known as andartes, had taken to the mountains and the hills, where resistance work was carried out. The two most important andarte bands were led by two former Greek army men — Ares (the name of the Greek god of war) Veloukhiotis, who was leader of ELAS (National People's Liberation Army) and Napoleon Zervas, leader of EDES (National Republican Greek League).

In 1942, when Myers and his men were parachuted into Greece, these bands were few in numbers. They had little arms and ammunition, little training and experience. They were poorly clothed and equipped. However, during the following two years, they grew in numbers, ELAS becoming the greater of the two. At the end of 1945 ELAS's strength was estimated at 20 000, with EDES at 5 000.

The Asopos Viaduct

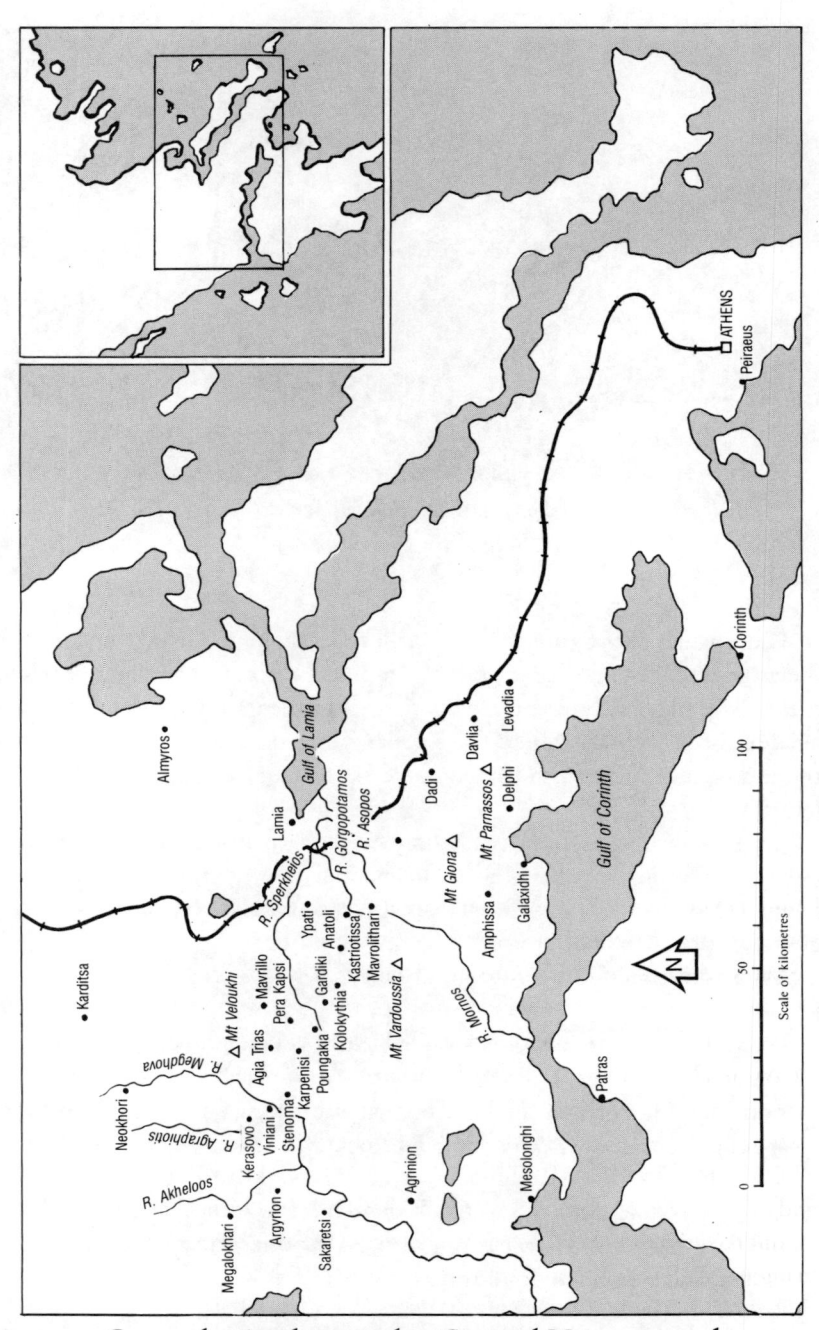

Greece, showing the area where Stott and Morton operated.

Brigadier Myers (right) with Napoleon Zervas, leader of EDES, in December 1942.

The British saboteurs received orders to stay in Greece and attach themselves to the guerilla forces. They received their arms and supplies from the Middle East, and these were distributed to the guerillas. Myers became head of the British Mission to the Greek Guerillas, as it was known, and by the end of 1944 the British Mission had 400 men of various nationalities on its staff.

After Myers had promoted Stott to Captain, he made contact with Geoffrey Gordon-Creed, who had landed safely, and was operating at Giona, north-west of Parnassus. Gordon-Creed was also trying to locate the guerilla leader Colonel Psaros.

About this time Stott wrote in his diary:

Today I met a famous Greek called Ares Veloukhiotis. He was the original leader of the Communist military group, and had just returned from a raid. He had about 200 men with him — some German prisoners, one New Zealander, and one British ex-POW. I wished these chaps luck, and told them everything would be all right, and not to worry. I told Ares not to touch these blokes, as they were British, and they would have to be taken before a British officer. Ares wished us luck and shook hands all round.

At this time in 1943, Ares led about 300 armed andartes, who were organised

The original British party dropped into Greece in the autumn of 1942. Those standing include Themie Marinos (first left), Chris Woodhouse (fourth left) and Brigadier Myers (fourth right). New Zealanders Arthur Edmonds and Tom Barnes are standing together (far right).

in bands of 25 each, scattered throughout the mountains.

M. B. McGlynn in his war history *Special Service in Greece* describes Ares as:

> . . . a small man, physically, and wiry. He had a long black beard, and usually wore a Cossack cap of black fur. Everything he did — moving and talking — was done quickly and spiritedly. His nose was small and hooked, and his eyes sharp and brown. From his wrist hung a vicious-looking leather whip. He described himself as a school teacher, and it was easily seen that he was well educated and also very intelligent. He could be pleasant, but his real nature was cold-hearted and cruel, and

in the manner of a fanatic was ruthless to anybody who stood in his way. He was a sadist and delighted in horrible forms of torturing and killing his victims. He was reputed to be homosexual, and to have served prison sentences for these offences.

All this time Stott had been unable to contact Colonel Psaros. However, he had managed to make contact with a young guerilla named Nikiphoros, who was one of Ares' youngest officers in ELAS. He was pro-British, brave and always had a very good fighting force with him. Dick Jones, the wireless operator who had parachuted in with him, was now with Gordon-Creed in Giona, so Stott was without a wireless set or operator. However, Brigadier Myers had promised he would send him a wireless operator as soon as he could, probably in the next moon period.

Stott's job now was to choose a good landing area in Parnassus, for the drop, and send Myers a map reference which would be sent on to Cairo. The stores would then be sent. A perfect landing area for the stores was selected, well under snow, and Stott sent a message, with a map, back to Myers with a Greek officer.

When the officer had gone, Stott was alone for the first time since he had arrived in Greece, and suddenly he felt the full weight of his responsibility. He established himself in Nikiphoros' village and lived with the local doctor for about 10 days. The doctor became a good friend to Stott, and although he was kind and helpful Stott decided that he must build a headquarters in the mountains, somewhere near the landing area, and away from the village. A village was too dangerous to live in. Greek peasants were routinely and indiscriminately shot, and their villages burned in reprisal every time a German was killed, or a train or bridge destroyed by resistance fighters. John Mulgan, who himself fought with the Greek resistance, writes in his *Report on Experience*:

> . . . peasant women, who, knowing that he was going down to the railway line to set charges, would load their donkeys with what they thought might be saved from the wrath to come.

Mulgan claims that the real heroes of the Greek war of resistance were 'the common people of the hills. It was on them, with their bitter, uncomplaining endurance, that the German terror broke. They produced no traitors.' The Greek people paid a terrible and disproportionate price for their resistance. They never surrendered or compromised, and as a result the Germans kept five divisions guarding Greece all through the War.

Chris Woodhouse, Themie Marinos and Don Stott.

Stott needed men now, particularly some who could speak English, and consequently was given a British soldier named Bill. Bill became his constant companion from then on, and acted as interpreter when necessary. In due course Stott and his men established themselves in their new quarters in the mountains, and waited for the long-promised planes with their stores. They built their signal fires and on a beautiful clear night heard the plane coming. They rushed out to light the fires, and the plane came down low to make its dropping run. Suddenly, to their horror, they realised that it was an enemy plane on the lookout for them, and bombs started to fall.

The guerillas ran off, and Bill, who had been out shooting rabbits and was drunk on wine when the bombs came, wandered around the area in a daze. He finally said 'Who threw those?' He helped Stott to put out the fires and then they made for the hills.

They waited and waited all that night and the next day but no more aircraft came. Stott and Bill were on their own, with no contact with anybody. As they were wondering what to do, a mysterious note was delivered by a Greek. It read: 'I hope this reaches you — I am giving it to this chap. I have heard that you are in the area here somewhere. Bob is with me.'

They assumed it was from Gordon-Creed. In the company of the Greek messenger, Stott walked for 30 hours across the mountains, and sure enough, met up with Gordon-Creed. But there was a wonderful surprise awaiting him. Bob Morton, now fit and well, ran out to greet him. The two old friends hugged each other. It seemed such a long time since they had seen each other.

There was more news: Gordon-Creed had found Colonel Psaros in another part of the Giona mountains. He had been in the north, whereas they were in the south. Stott was now able to send all his messages to Cairo. Morton was keen to return with Stott, so they decided to return together to Parnassus. Psaros was later killed by ELAS after the dissolution of his regiment on 16 April 1944.

Stott and Morton quickly earned the reputation of being absolutely fearless, and willing to take on any task. They were establishing a reputation as the most daring and resourceful of the special service agents in Greece.

It was now May 1943, and the British Military Mission was firmly established, with key men planted everywhere in Greece. Brigadier Myers thought that there would be enough forces now to blow up the Asopos railway viaduct, in eastern Roumeli. This viaduct was high on Mt Vardoussia above the Gulf of Corinth, with a magnificent view of the Oiti, Giona and Vardoussia mountains. Two hundred metres in length, it was a vital link in Hitler's war supply line between Salonika and Athens. The viaduct was suspended between two tunnels over a precipitous chasm 100 m deep, through which a rushing torrent raged. It was heavily guarded and even the tough Greek guerillas considered it impregnable. At night the whole area was swept by searchlights. Being close to the ELAS headquarters, it was centrally situated for operations, and yet was secure from attack, as the nearest road was six hours away.

Myers instructed Lt Colonel Arthur Edmonds, the New Zealander who was Liaison Officer in charge of the area, to start planning for the destruction of the 'Soapy One', as it was code-named. Myers gave a new code-name — 'Washing' — to the proposed operation. Three English sapper officers, Pat Wingate, Kenneth Scott and Harry McIntyre, were already on their way into Greece to assist with the demolition.

During May 1943, Stott and Morton, in the company of Geoffrey Gordon-Creed and Lt Colonel Edmonds, and the three sappers, attended a meeting to discuss the possibilities of blowing the viaduct. They were told that if the viaduct was blown, German communications would be cut for at least six months. Edmonds had already reconnoitred the area, and proposed that 1000 guerillas be used to waylay the German garrison guarding the viaduct. The sabotage party could then move in and destroy the bridge.

It seemed a perfect plan. It was practised by the saboteurs, and the charges had already been made when, three days before the event was to take place, word came through from guerilla headquarters that they could not take part in the operation. EAM, the political division of ELAS, had ruled that its army was not to be used in the operation.

Stott was lying in bed one night when he said to Gordon-Creed: 'We can do it ourselves!'

The approach to the bridge in one direction was through a long tortuous gorge. This gorge was claimed to be impassable, and Stott reckoned it would not be guarded. His plan was to go through the gorge, climb up from underneath the bridge, plant the explosives, put time fuses or pencils on, and get away. All this would have to be done in freezing water, over rapids, and waterfalls which at times showed a sheer drop of 30 m.

Stott and Gordon-Creed approached Myers with this idea. 'Well, I was hoping that someone would come forward with a feasible idea,' said Myers. 'Go ahead, boys, and reconnoitre the area.'

The bridge, however, proved worse than its reputation. Above it the cliffs rose 300 m, forcing the men into the icy water. There were treacherous rapids, and the walls were high and sheer. They would need ropes and special climbing equipment. The men reported back to Brigadier Myers that a 20-metre waterfall, a short distance inside the chasm, had stopped them. Every available piece of parachute rigging was collected, and plaited into ropes thick enough to grasp.

On 21 May Stott took into the gorge another party of volunteers — Gordon-Creed, Morton, the three sapper officers, Wingate, Scott and McIntyre, Lance-Corporal Chester Lockwood, an escaped British POW and a Greek interpreter and guide, George Karadjopoulos. They carried

The rugged terrain of the Asopos Gorge.

gym shoes with them to wear on entering the gorge, from which point onwards they would travel unarmed except for rubber 'coshes'. Their chances of success depended on their ability to remain unobserved by the Germans.

They gradually made their way through the gorge, getting a little further every day. It was agonising progress, and Stott recalled later that he had never been involved in anything as tough. The place was alive with scorpions and centipedes, the water was freezing cold, there were high waterfalls and rocks falling down all the time. The men had to carry high explosives, and keep them out of the water. Stott was nominated by Gordon-Creed as leader of the expedition, and he planned the actual approach to the bridge.

They had gone about a kilometre into the gorge, when they reached a place that was impassable. Water rushed through it like a sheet, and down a sheer drop into a deep pool. There was no place to tie a rope, and if they had slipped, they would have gone straight into the pool and drowned. The fact that they could not get any further sapped the men's morale.

However, Stott reacted differently, and was more determined than ever to get through the gorge. He had been the only one who had believed that they could get through, and he had to live up to his words. At this stage some of the men tried to back out of the operation, so Stott and Morton decided they would go it alone. They decided to make one last effort and agreed that if they could not do it that day they would cancel the whole operation.

They climbed to a height of about 50 m along the side of the sheer face of the gorge, and as Stott clung to a branch of scrub his footing suddenly gave way and he swung over the gorge by one hand. That shook him so much that he knew they could not get explosives through there. He had noticed, however, a flat ledge about half way up where a large tree was growing. If they could get up to the ledge, chop down the tree, trim off the branches, and drop it into the gorge, they could use it like a ladder. But they had no axes.

Bitterly disappointed, the two men went back to headquarters, and orders came through to cancel the operation to allow the party time to recuperate. It was just as well, for the men were covered with cuts and bruises, and generally suffering from exposure.

While waiting for ropes, grappling irons, and other equipment from Cairo, the men were sent off to different areas to reconnoitre and select targets which were to be attacked by the andartes in a general operation, named 'Animals'. The purpose of this operation was to divert and occupy the enemy while the Allies landed in Sicily. Morton, who knew the Athens area well, was selected to go there on the important and hazardous assignment of surveying the aerodrome defences; this was the first step in a plan to destroy the aircraft on the ground. Unfortunately this operation, which involved a double-agent, nearly ended in disaster. Morton had to order his newly assembled andarte band to disperse and save themselves.

When in Athens he concentrated on assigning agents to various jobs, while he set about attacking another viaduct — a large, strongly guarded, steel bridge. He took only one Greek with him. Hidden on the bridge, they waited until an ammunition train filled with troops appeared. With the train only 300 metres away they set the charges. The operation was successful and the wreckage blocked the line for eight days. For this action, Morton won the DCM. His citation reads:

> His personality and courage made him a favourite with foreign people with whom he worked, thereby keeping the prestige of the British at a high level . . .

Unfortunately Morton was not back in time to be included in the party for the final assault on the viaduct, and Stott was deeply disappointed in not having him along.

On 15 June, Stott, in the company of Driver Charlie Mutch of the New Zealand 4th RMT (Reserve Mechanical Transport), and a Palestinian Arab soldier, Khouri, left the village of Anatoli loaded up with climbing gear. The plan was for them to press through to the viaduct, and then send for Gordon-Creed, Scott and McIntyre. They duly climbed up the side of the gorge, cut down the tree, and made it into a perfect ladder. Stott took the rope and finally arrived at the bridge site. He lay on his stomach, and he could see the Germans painting the bridge. He was now almost right underneath it. Keeping his eye on the guard walking across the viaduct, he made a dash from rock to rock, watching the bridge the whole time. Fortunately, the guard did not see him. Not 5 m away, two Germans stood washing their socks. He had no cover at all, as he was standing in the middle of the river, and if he had been seen, the whole operation would have been ruined. He returned to the others, who were waiting anxiously for him. He quickly wrote out a note, and gave it to Sergeant Mutch to take back to Colonel Edmonds. It read:

> I was able to get down the big waterfall, found it was the last, and suddenly, when I rounded the bend, I came face to face with 'Mrs Washing' herself! There was a lot of activity going on, and workmen

were swarming over the viaduct, strengthening it to carry heavier loads, and making a deuce of a din, rivetting I think. They have scaffolding erected all over it, and ladders leading up from the bottom. I was taking all this in when I looked down at the stream, and saw two workmen only about 10 yards away from me, working with their heads down, getting stones out of the stream. Luckily they didn't see me, and I quickly got out of sight. These workmen came down from the railway line by some steps cut in the north cliff side, and we should be able to get up this way. Please send Geoff, Scotty and Mac immediately. The job's in the bag. I am going off on a recce of the road south of Lamia while the others are coming.

Yours, Don.

In the meantime, Gordon-Creed had written a note to Edmonds: 'I think it is silly carrying on with the bridge — the whole thing is impracticable. We would never get to the bridge.'

Stott's note to Edmonds arrived about an hour before Gordon-Creed's.

McIntyre, Scott and Gordon-Creed reached the lead party on 18 June. In the meantime, Stott had made a further reconnaisance of the gorge, and estimated the garrison strength. He saw that there were searchlights at many vantage points, and that while the workmen toiled they were protected by a guard of about 35 men. On 19 June they reached the place where they had dropped the tree in the gorge, and there they prepared the charges. There was no question now as to who was in command.

The following night, 20 June, the men stood shoulder deep in freezing water in the moonlight until midnight, and then moved in. Stott again crawled up the track on his stomach. He told the others to wait until he had been to the base of the bridge, and then the remainder of the party were to follow. The men crawled along the scaffolding to the point where they were to blow the bridge. The garrison building was only 50 m away from where they were working, and two of the guards were walking up and down overhead, not more than 10 to 12 metres above where Stott was. He sat on the girder and applied 50 kg of plastic explosive, and then gave the saboteurs the nod, one by one, to lay the charges.

Gordon-Creed was left at the base of the bridge on guard. He had not been there long when he saw a German guard approaching. To have got so far, and for this to happen now! The men froze in the shadow of the viaduct. Gordon-Creed signalled to the two sapper officers to keep quiet, then hid himself by the track. The German came nearer and nearer, and just when he was in front of him. Gordon-Creed jumped out of hiding, grabbed him, and hit him over the head as hard as he could with a piece of wood. The German dropped without a sound, and Gordon-Creed threw him over the gorge into the rushing water below. He whispered to the sappers: 'For God's sake, be quick.'

The Asopos Viaduct, later destroyed in a daring raid on 20 June 1943.

A searchlight swung from one end of the viaduct to the other, but apparently no sound had been picked up by the Germans. Machine-gun posts were planted all around them, and Stott and his men had to be extra careful. Would their luck hold? The sappers set their time pencils for a 30-minute delay, and every move had to be done slowly and carefully. They used the shadows to the best advantage, and finally everything was finished. It was then just on midnight, and the charges had been fixed to the four members of the arch, connected with rings of explosive fuse and duplicated. The fuse was set for 1.30 a.m. but the bridge did not blow up until 2.05 in the morning. By that time Stott was going back through the gorge when he heard the explosion and saw the flash, but he could not be sure what had happened at that stage.

Unable to contain himself any longer, Stott was the first one, typically, to hoist himself to a vantage point up the gorge, 300 m above the bridge. In the distance he could hear orders shouted to the German soldiers, and the sound of gushing water. It was difficult for him to make out what had actually happened. He had to rub his eyes to see that he wasn't dreaming. My God! Every scrap of the viaduct was gone. The physical and nervous strain of the previous 24 hours made him wonder if he was seeing things.

He waited there until just before dawn, and as the sunlight gradually came into the gorge he could see the whole viaduct lying in its side at the bottom. He then made his way carefully back to base camp.

By now the German patrols were looking everywhere for the saboteurs, and it was dangerous to lurk in the area for too long. At the camp the men were jubilant at their success. They had done the impossible! The result of the mission was immediately reported to General Headquarters, Middle East. Subsequent air photographs proved the viaduct to be completely destroyed.

The Germans were infuriated by what had happened, but were convinced that it was impossible for enemy raiding parties to have achieved this object. Consequently, they accused their own garrison of gross neglect and sabotage and, as a result, the Commanding Officer and the entire garrison were shot by firing squad.

The demolition of Asopos was regarded as one of the war's best sabotage feats. Both Colonel Edmonds and Brigadier Myers recommended Stott for the Victoria Cross, but because there had not been any shots fired he eventually received the DSO, as did Gordon-Creed. Of course, if shots had been fired, the game would have been well and truly given away. Scott and McIntyre each received the MC, Mutch the MM and Khouri a bar to his MM.

Colonel Chris Woodhouse, DSO OBE, who was Myers' Second-in-Command, and who succeeded Myers as Head of the British Mission to Greece, adds:

> The object of the operation, which cut the German communications for about six weeks in July 1943, along with dozens of others simultaneously, was to convince the Germans that the Allies' next target after clearing North Africa was to be mainland Greece. (In reality it was, of course, Sicily.)
>
> The whole exercise worked beautifully: Hitler ordered six divisions from the Russian front into the Balkans, though only two actually reached Greece. The destruction of the Asopos Viaduct made it impossible for the Germans to get out again by rail, so they were limited to road transport on the most horrendous roads in Europe.
>
> There is not much more that I can add about Don Stott, except that he was the bravest man I ever knew. But that will do.

CHAPTER 3

Rendezvous with the Germans

'Death seemed my servant on the road, till we were near and saw you waiting: When you smiled, and in sorrowful envy he outran me and took you apart: Into his quietness.'

T. E. LAWRENCE

On 23 July 1943, not long after the Asopos exploit, Stott was ordered to stage an immediate sabotage attempt on German aircraft on the Tatoi, Kalamaki, Megara, and Elevsis airfields near Athens. Stott realised that he could not rely on the local guerillas, so he sent Morton and his old friend, Bill, who had been with him in the Parnassus mountains, to Athens to contact approximately 50 men.

In the meantime Stott was told that a certain highway, which was going to be used by the German and Italian troops to fight in the Sicilian campaign, must be sabotaged. He made a reconnaissance of the area, and selected a bridge and built-up portion of the road in the form of a culvert, which he intended to destroy. General Headquarters in Cairo was to send over special aeroplane bombs, and also two Captains, who were experts in that kind of demolition work.

Stott shifted his headquarters from Parnassus to Desphina, where he would receive the stores and men. On the night of 4 August, in the company again of Sergeant Charlie Mutch who had helped to blow up the Asopos Viaduct, and some shepherds, he blew up the bridge, and then moved to the more difficult culvert. It took Stott until 2 a.m. to lay the charges in the culvert. He finally gave the order: 'Everything going to be blown!' and then set the fuse. About five minutes later, up she went! Stott lifted his head too soon to see what damage had been done, and was badly wounded in the side of his head. He saw an enormous hole in the ground, which held up reinforcements being moved into Albania, and on to Italy, for the opening of the Sicilian campaign. This held up 463 vehicles for 12 days.

Stott and his men quickly moved away from the area. Stott, by now in great pain, rode a mule all night to meet Bob Morton and 50 other men. Somehow he managed to reach the meeting place he had arranged with Morton, although he was a day late. However, no one was there, and later he learned that the Germans had attacked the men, and they had been forced to flee.

Stott had no idea where to find Morton, and all but one of the guerillas had gone. He knew that General Headquarters in Cairo expected the aerodromes outside Athens to be attacked by 10 August. There he was with the aeroplane bombs and arms, and only himself and one Greek guerilla to attack the aerodromes, which were heavily guarded by the Germans.

Stott, being not in the least inclined to give in to any disability, decided he would have a go at the aeordromes, or one of them, himself. He sent a wireless message to Cairo, asking whether it would be possible to delay the operation. Cairo replied that the operation would have to be cancelled unless the target was attacked on the 10th, as the objective was to stop any Stukas, which were being used in the Sicilian campaign, taking off from the aerodromes. It was now after the 20th, so the whole operation was cancelled.

By this time Stott's head had swollen to the size of a pumpkin, and he was nearly crazy with the pain. He sent the Greek guerilla through to Athens, in the hope that he might be able to bring back a doctor. Luckily the guerilla found a doctor, and early the following morning the doctor arrived. He immeidately relieved the pressure, but told Stott he would have to go into Athens for a further operation. It would be fatal to wait any longer.

It took three days for Stott to walk to Athens, as by now he was almost delirious. Reaching the outskirts of the city, he waited for dusk, and struggled into the uniform of a British officer — shorts, bush shirt, boots, and a bandage around his head.

In the centre of Athens lived an ear, nose and throat specialist, who happened to be a very good friend of Stott's. Fortunately he was at home, but he was most concerned over the state of Stott's health, and said that he would have to operate immediately. However, the only hospital available was a private maternity home so Stott, in the company of the specialist, hobbled the 300 m or so to the hospital. In next to no time, he had received a shot of morphine and a local anaesthetic. The operation took three-quarters of an hour, and he was conscious throughout.

The specialist was concerned that Stott would try and leave as soon as he could walk again, so he insisted that he stay in the hospital for at least three days. Stott was quite happy to do so, and enjoyed the enforced convalescence. The maternity home overlooked the main street of Athens, and he would watch the Germans patrolling up and down.

On the third night he moved to a friend's house. Somehow or other, word got out that Stott was in town, and it became too dangerous to stay in Athens any longer. He was still weak and ill after his operation, but he decided he would have to get out of the city, and return to the Desphina headquarters.

Desphina was a 24-hour walk away, across the mountains behind Athens. Stott was so tired he would walk for a short distance, and then suddenly find himself flat on the ground. He would sleep for five minutes, and then walk for another two or three hours, before falling asleep again. He came to a village, and rested there for four hours. He hired a mule after that, and moved on from village to village, finally arriving back at the monastery — his old headquarters at Desphina. As he rode down the path, he could see the welcome figure of Bob Morton rushing up to greet him, with several Greeks all talking excitedly. Willing hands lifted him off the mule as the world around him spun in front of his eyes.

When he had recovered, Stott decided that the aerodromes outside Athens must be attacked again. Despite having been ordered not to go into Athens alone again, he left Morton behind to organise agents inside the aerodrome, and set off for Athens. He had gone only a short distance when a frantic guerilla told him that the Germans were moving in on the Desphina headquarters. They raced back, collected all their belongings, and moved to Helicon Mountains.

By this time, Captain Harry McIntyre had become permanently attached to Stott as Saboteur Officer. The men had not been in their new headquarters long when confirmation came that the Germans had moved in on Desphina. Traitors had told the Germans that Stott had been there on numerous occasions, and consequently nine hostages were taken, one of whom was the doctor who had first dressed Stott's head.

Stott refers to the village of Desphina in his diary as a place where he would often stay a night at a time, and live with a rather well-to-do married couple:

> They were always pleased to see me, even though I turned up in grimy old shorts, a pistol round my waist with a couple of grenades, and with long hair. When the Germans came, the husband made for the hills, and left the wife to face the music. She was a most attractive woman,

and she invited the German officers in to have tea. German officers were charmed by beautiful women, but when they found out later that she had entertained me, the woman was arrested.

Stott located the woman, and decided to rescue her. It was risky, but he thought it was worth a good try. He took McIntyre with him, and they walked into the village, right under the noses of the German guards. They found the woman, collected her belongings, and smuggled her out of the village. They took her to their headquarters in the mountains, where she was joined four or five days later by her very frightened husband.

About this time Don spent some time with Chris Woodhouse, who had become a good friend. 'We spent several days together in the late summer of 1943,' says Woodhouse, 'about which I recall only the endless laughter after each successful operation. Bob Morton was also with Don at the time, and I can truthfully say that I never had any more delightful war-time companions.

'I can still hear Don's voice in my mind — pure New Zealand — slightly more rasping than English, much gentler than Australian, and always with a latent humour below the surface.'

By October 1943 the war had reached a critical stage for the Germans. Russia, America and Britain had made a pact to 'collaborate in war and peace'. The quisling Mayor of Athens, Angelos Georgatos, who was friendly with the Germans, and yet known to have sympathies with the British, approached Stott and asked him to a meeting with the Germans to discuss proposals for peace. Stott was dubious about this, understandably, so he asked another agent to check it out. It proved to be correct. Apparently the Germans realised that as the war on the Eastern Front was going badly for them, and as Italy had capitulated, the odds were stacked heavily against them.

Georgatos let it be known that Gestapo Captain Haiz Schumann wanted to contact a British officer as he hoped that, if suitable terms could be reached with the British, Germany would be able to concentrate on Russia, as Russia was considered a far greater menace. Schumann admitted to Georgatos that 'we are in a sorry plight'.

Later Stott wrote about these 'peace feelers' between himself and the Germans. He gives three reasons why he agreed to the meeting with Schumann and Georgatos:

> After checking details about Schumann and the Mayor, I decided I would meet the Germans' representative for several reasons:
> 1. Felt Germany had something to say.

2. If Germans offered (peace) I would not accept, but hoped by meeting them to get current German thoughts and ideas.
3. Also keen to return to Cairo to report and hoped the Germans might grant a safe passage.

In due course a rendezvous was arranged, preparations being most elaborate. It took place on 13 November 1943 on waste land near Kifissia (a suburb in Athens), surrounded by agents well armed in support. Stott arranged for his interpreter, who worked at German Headquarters, to be there also, and left one agent to bring a German representative with the Mayor. Stott wasn't satisfied with the situation, and left Bob Morton to sort everything out. Morton met the German representative and the Mayor in a car, and brought them to the rendezvous where Stott waited in full British uniform. This was to create the impression that he had just come in from the mountains, and had not been in the city area.

The rendezvous was at 9 p.m. Captain Schumann and the Mayor arrived both visibly alarmed when they saw Stott in uniform, backed up by 'evil-looking agents', as Stott described them in his diary. Schumann asked if they could go somewhere else, saying there was much to talk about, so Stott agreed to go to their rendezvous — the Mayor's flat. Stott had a feeling that the Germans were sincere, but he cetainly wasn't going to take any chances. Schumann remained with the sapper officer as hostage, whilst Stott went with the Mayor to meet the Gestapo head of south-eastern Europe, Colonel Loss, and the diplomatic representative, Wellun.

Bob Morton was Stott's bodyguard and Stott drove them all in the Mayor's car to Georgatos's flat, which was in the most populated part of Athens. The Mayor's flat was on the fourth floor, and when they had all arrived, Wellun, whom Stott had never met before, threw Stott a salute and seemed to be visibly taken aback at Stott in full British uniform. Wellun, 18 stone and typically Prussian in appearance, was in civilian clothes.

They all shook hands. Mayor Georgatos suggested Black and White whisky as a toast, and then there was an embarrassed silence.

'Well, gentlemen,' said Georgatos, 'Good luck!'

This was echoed by Wellun and Loss as 'goot lock!' They fenced around for a while, but suddenly the ice was broken. 'I have no diplomatic status,' said Stott. 'If you have anything to say, please say it, and I will act as agent in Cairo.'

The Germans deliberated, and then decided to discuss the matter with Loss's superior, Hermann Neubacher, who was Hitler's special envoy to the Balkans. Stott and his men were asked to remain at the Mayor's flat. It was plain now that the whole affair was supposed to be highly secret, and that the German Army was not supposed to know anything about it.

During their discussion, the Germans asked for an interpreter, so Stott sent for a young Greek friend of his who worked at German Headquarters during the day. He was 23 years of age, and had been an Athens College graduate. Stott suggested to him that he should appear in disguise, and when he entered the Mayor's flat, he was dressed as a fisherman, together with a sweeping moustache.

'Guten Abend,' he greeted the Germans. 'Good evening,' he said to Stott.

The Germans eyed him with amused silence.

'What is your name?' Stott asked him.

'I don't think that is of any importance,' said the young Greek.

Stott suppressed a chuckle at this, as the Greek had been living with him for the previous six weeks. 'You had better put your beard back in position!' Stott told him. 'It has become unstuck.'

The whole thing was ludicrous, and the Germans could scarcely contain their amusement.

'Ah! He is disguised!' said Georgatos.

'Obviously,' said Colonel Loss, and roared with laughter.

Later during the meeting, the Greek's beard stuck to a glass and became completely unhinged. He decided to abandon it altogether, and clung to his false moustache only.

Whilst the Germans had been absent, Stott had been most relieved to find one of his most faithful agents hidden behind a screen covering the Germans with a .45 calibre gun.

At 11.30 that night the Germans said that the final decision must rest with 'Der Führer'. Stott continues the story:

> They asked me if I would remain in contact with them for 10 days, while they flew to Berlin and back. Since I was now in it up to my neck, I agreed. They decided Captain Schumann should be left at my disposal, so that anything I requested would be given. They promised that I would be safe, including all my men.
>
> Loss struck me as a gentleman, and a man I could trust. But I was not so sure about Wellun. I didn't think I could trust him. I decided too, that sooner than involve my group, I would stay in the Mayor's flat. It is interesting to note that while staying at the flat we lived on the most wonderful food imaginable in a city where more had died of starvation than any other. How and where he [Georgatos] scrounged food is a mystery.

I had a great ambition to look at the famous Corinth Bridge and Defence Zone. This had never been seen by a British officer, to my knowledge, since the beginning of the German occupation. Several times parties had been sent to blow the bridge, but had failed because it was fiercely protected.

I decided to test the German sincerity, so I requested Captain Schumann to allow a visit to the mountain area to pick up some planted stores. I also asked to be allowed transport, knowing full well that the only way was via the Corinth Bridge. He immediately agreed.

Stott went into the hills to his secret wireless station, found the set out of order and returned to the German escort. On his conducted trip through the Corinth Canal he took particular notice of the roads, railways and defence around the canal. Later he was able to put this to good use when he informed General Headquarters in Cairo, and the British were able to attack the enemy installations in that area.

Captain Henry McIntyre, Chris Woodhouse and Don Stott discuss plans. On the right is a Greek interpreter, Allen Sotirakopoulos.

Some people believed that Stott's 'peace feelers' were an 'antagonistic' game between the British Secret Information Services of Army Headquarters, Middle East, and Stott himself. Others believed that the efforts of the New Zealand Captain were against the Greek EAM guerilla organisation, and that he was doing his best to assist in a political solution for the liberation of Greece. Spiros Kotsis, author of *Midas 614*, writes:

> The only people who know what really happened are the British. Many officers of large German units were ready to defect, and together with Loss had the order to negotiate exclusively with the British because they did not trust either of the guerilla movements. Loss offered himself as hostage — a guarantee to his word in the agreement. Finally, the meeting closed with the decision that Stott was to convey these decisions personally to the Middle East Headquarters, and to return with a responsible reply.

In my research and talks with Chris Woodhouse, Brigadier Myers and Sir Peter Wilkinson, one of the heads of SOE, it would seem that Stott acted mainly on his own in his negotiations with the Germans, save for one British officer, Brigadier C. M. Keble, head of SOE in Cairo in 1943-44. It is known that Keble was extremely unpopular, but he did have an ability to go straight to the heart of problems. He encouraged Stott in the 'peace feelers' negotiations, a fact confirmed by Sir Peter Wilkinson, who was in Cairo at the time. Wilkinson states that matters of that kind could only be handled by British Liaison Officers on the specific instructions of Ministers. Wilkinson told Keble further that all negotiations must be broken off, if they had already started, and that SOE London be informed of all the circumstances. Keble replied that he had complete confidence and faith in the officer concerned.

Dominque Eudes, author of *The Kapetanios: Partisans and Civil War in Greece, 1943-1949*, says that Hermann Neubacher stated in his memoirs that 'proposals were made by certain British officers present in Athens at the beginning of the winter of 1943'. No names are mentioned, and the following report appears in Neubacher's *Sonderauftrag Sudost*:

> This war should end in a common struggle by the Allies and the German forces against Bolshevism . . . This is not yet the official opinion of His Majesty's Government or of Middle East HQ in Cairo, but it is the view held by a number of important officers at Middle East HQ. These officers see clearly that Communist infiltration is already a serious threat to the whole Mediterranean region, and they think that their point of view could soon become the official British attitude. It is regrettable that the Communist partisans in Greece should still be receiving British support in the form of arms and money (actually

ELAS had received no British aid since the end of October, 1943) . . . it may be possible to correct this state of things by sending arms to anti-Communist groups by submarine . . . Are the Germans ready to hold official talks on this matter?

Eudes says that when Stott returned to Cairo he was actually tried in front of a military tribunal, but according to Panayotis Rongakos, who was present at the trial, Stott was not only acquitted but warmly congratulated by his superiors.

There is no doubt that Stott had the best interests of the Greeks at heart. The future of the Greeks was his main concern. This is backed up by author Zalo Koetas, in his book *Chronicles of Occupied Greece*. One passage reads:

> I met Don Stott four months after he became Liaison Officer of the Attikis/Boeotias district. He came from Ellikana Hills to study how to save the Greek capital from falling into the hands of Communists. The presence of Stott resolved the differences in one night.

On 21 November, Loss arrived back from Berlin and asked Stott to return to Cairo with agreement feelers for a local peace in Greece. Stott agreed to do this. On 23 November, Stott left Greece, reaching Chios the following day. The German Commander of the island arranged Stott's safe passage into Turkey, and he arrived in Cairo a few days later.

Nothing came of the peace feelers. There is no concrete evidence to say what really happened when Stott arrived back in Cairo, but it is very likely these 'peace feelers' were rejected on the spot by the British. This assumption would appear to be correct, as it is known that some of the British SOE officers were far from impressed with Stott's actions. Colonel Chris Woodhouse, the British officer who replaced Brigadier Myers as head of the British Military Mission in Greece, in his book on Greek politics, *Apple of Discord*, mentions the fact that the British authorities immediately cancelled the negotiations as soon as Stott returned to Cairo. He writes:

> Captain Stott, a New Zealand officer, entered Athens in the autumn of 1943, to carry out sabotage. His courage and originality soon involved him in other, far more perilous activities, in the process of which his political associations were largely of the extreme right. One of them was General Papagos, Chief of the General Staff of the Greek Army under Metaxis in 1940–41.
>
> Another far less inoffensive person was the Mayor of Athens who

had been installed by the Germans. Through the latter he found himself entering into negotiations of a complicated nature with the German occupation authorities. These communications were abruptly severed when they came to the notice of higher British authorities, who had not, at first, understood their gravity.

Stott was later to receive a Bar to his DSO for the 'peace overtures', which some historians refer to as 'thankless'.

In the words of the citation:

His life was at the mercy of the Germans throughout, and at no time did he give any information to the enemy about our own very extensive set-up in Greece. Our own knowledge of the Germans and a great deal of useful intelligence was gained by him during these contacts. Our chances of attacking the Athens airfields successfully at a later date were much enhanced by the underground organisation which he set up there, and the information he gained during his tour under German guidance enabled operations to be planned against the road and railway between Athens and Corinth.

CHAPTER 4

Preparation for Borneo

*What a time Charon has chosen to take you,
Now when the branches are blossoming and the earth putting out grass.*

GREEK RIZITIKA FOR THE DEATH OF THE HERO DIAKOS, 1824

Stott arrived in England some time before the invasion of Europe on D-day, 6 June 1944. He was asked to lecture to much higher-ranking officers than himself on the hazards of the operations in Greece. It was at one of these meetings that a high-ranking American officer, who was in private life a Hollywood film producer, asked him if he would sell him his life story. Stott was rather amused at this. He seemed to think that what he had done did not qualify for a film to be made.

It was while he was in England that he was offered a Staff job which he refused. The thought of sitting behind a desk after all he had been through was too much for him. He would much rather remain in the field of operations. When a job with the Far East Zone was suggested, he accepted, knowing he would be able to get some home leave.

Don Stott returned to New Zealand and his home in Birkenhead in May 1944 with a DSO & Bar. During the time he had been away, several newspapers had written about his exploits, and he had become something of a national hero. However, he wasn't interested in praise or adulation. He was more concerned with helping the Greeks, and he was worried about the fate of some of his Greek friends.

His niece, Barbara Lewis, has vivid memories of her uncle at this time: 'When Uncle Don returned home after the war, he was restless, often pacing the floor at my grandmother's home. He had been through so much that life in sleepy Birkenhead must have seemed very tame after Greece.'

Don Stott's wedding to Mary Snow in June 1944. The wedding dress was made from the parachute Stott used in Greece. Keith Simcock, Stott's best man, is on the left.

In June, about a month after his return to New Zealand, Stott married his childhood sweetheart, Mary Snow. Mary was the daughter of the local Birkenhead constable, and she and Stott had corresponded frequently during Stott's time overseas. Edna Meehan, Mary's sister, remembers him vividly:

> We all thought Don was wonderful. He had a great personality and a most forceful one. He would liven up the dullest party within two minutes of his entering the room. He was very romantic and literally swept Mary off her feet.

They were married at St Patrick's Cathedral in Auckland on a beautiful fine but cold winter's day. Mary's silk wedding dress had been made from the parachute that Don had carefully preserved all the time he was in Greece and brought back to New Zealand. Bob Morton had been unable to attend the wedding, as he had not returned yet from Greece.

Keith Simcock, now a doctor and living in Auckland, was Stott's best man at the wedding.

'I still have such a vivid picture today of that wedding,' he says. 'Mary, stunningly beautiful in her wedding gown and radiant with happiness, and Don — tall and thin and so alive with that special aura around him. After the service, we all walked down Queen St, laughing and joking, and not a care in the world. Stott had a vitality about him — a certain charisma, which attracted people to him. He was dedicated to playing the game, and winning it. I don't think it ever occurred to him that he could die on this last trip of his, and I think we all felt the same way. He was indestructible somehow.

How I wish I had been able to spend more time with him. He left an imprint on my life I will never forget.'

Stott was unable to tell his family much about his impending operation in the Far East. According to his brother, Bob, his main objective when he came back from Greece was to assemble a group of experienced men to go into an area where the Japanese were. He went to the War Office in Wellington to recruit some men, and the men he had known overseas all turned him down, as they considered they were not in his class.

One man who did not turn him down was Harry Cotterill. Cotterill had fought and trained with a commando unit in Australia as early as 1940. He was set to go into Borneo with Stott, and plans were made for his wife, Nancy, a close friend of Mary's, to stay in Melbourne with Mary until the time came for both men to go to Borneo. This never eventuated, for Cotterill failed his medical. Instead, Leslie McMillan, known as 'Mac', went in place of Cotterill.

'Don told me this was definitely going to be his last sortie,' Cotterill says. 'He regarded the trip to Borneo as a piece of cake. He thought it would be so easy compared to his previous jobs in Greece.'

Stott's mother naturally worried about him. She had just got her son safely back, and now she was going to lose him again.

'Don't worry, Mum,' he told her. 'This is going to be my last job, and when I come home it will be for good, I promise.'

John Stott, Don's nephew, remembers his uncle spending much time with him when he came back to New Zealand. 'He had a wonderful gift for drawing and entertained us with his cartoon impressions. I was so proud of him, and I look back on those times as precious.'

Stott would often remark to his family that he hoped more than anything that none of his young nephews would ever be involved in any more wars.

Stott was duly sent to Melbourne where he was to undergo an intensive training course. In the meantime, Bob Morton had arrived back in New

Zealand, and while in Auckland visited the Stotts. Morton also had been accepted for 'special duties' and, as he and Stott were told later, this was to be in Japanese-occupied Borneo.

Just after this, Stott sent a letter home to his parents. 'Bob's arrival was a great surprise,' he wrote. 'I was thrilled to meet up with him again. It brought back many happy memories. I suppose by this time he has been to see you. I warned him that the Stotts of Birkenhead are just ordinary folk, and that if he stayed at our place he would be accepted as one of the family.'

Stott and Morton were both now 'on loan' to the Australian Army as experts on Special Service work, and seconded to the Services Reconnaissance Department, known as SRD. They were attached to 'Z' Special Unit, a highly secret force of commandoes and saboteurs. By this time, Stott was a Major and Morton a Captain with a DCM. The Australians took notice of what they said.

Mary Stott, who was expecting their first child, accompanied Don to Melbourne, and when it was time for the men to go into Borneo she returned to New Zealand. She gave birth to a son, Geoffrey, in March.

Stott's widow and son Geoffrey at the presentation at Government House, Auckland, of the Bar to Stott's DSO. Left to right: General Freyberg, Annie Stott (Don's mother), Lady Freyberg, Geoffrey, Mary Stott, Robert Stott (Don's father).

Stott received the news of the birth a few days before he and the other 'Z' operatives left on their highly-secret mission to Borneo. He was ecstatic and he had expressed a wish to Mary before she had left to return to New Zealand that if they had a son he would like him to be named Geoffrey, after Geoffrey Gordon-Creed, with whom he had worked in Greece.

Stott's mission to Borneo was named Robin 1, and its men consisted of New Zealanders, Australians, Indonesians and one Malay interpreter. They were:

Major D. J. Stott DSO & Bar — Commanding Officer (NZ)
Captain L. T. McMillan — Second-in-Command (NZ)
Lieutenant W. C. Dwyer (Australia)
Warrant Officer R. G. Houghton (NZ)
Sergeant W. Horrocks (NZ)
Private Kondoy Satu (Indonesia)
Captain R. M. Morton MC, DCM (NZ)
Warrant Officer L. Farquharson (Australia)
Sergeant B. Dooland (Australia)
Sergeant R. L. Dey (Indonesia)
Private Kondoy Dua (Indonesia)
Sergeant Bin Ali (Malay Interpreter)

The Robin 1 party left Perth in the US submarine *Perch* under the command of Commander Blish Hills on 12 March 1945. The *Perch* had some 2 600 kg of stores, of which 560 kg were signals equipment. Folboats and rubber boats were lashed to the outside of the submarine hull and were carried in this manner when submerged. Blish Hills set his course for Borneo — Balikpapan Bay via Surabaya, Lombok Strait, Flores Sea, Java Sea, and the Strait of Makasar leading to the dropping zone.

During the uneventful, but somewhat cramped voyage, the boats were unlashed from the hull and assembled from time to time when the submarine was on the surface. On these occasions it was found that a certain amount of water had penetrated through the valves of the rubber boats, which had to be removed before they could be launched. The outboard motors, which were carried inside the submarine, were also tried out during the voyage.

As the submarine approached its dropping zone area on the morning of 20 March, Stott, McMillan, Dooland and Horrocks, the four operatives who were to be inserted into Balikpapan as a first party to reconnoitre the area, began to feel tense and nervous. Their hearts beat fast as the submarine lay submerged during the daylight hours, and Stott called a conference to run over the final operational orders, for it was most important that everybody

Stott at a training camp in Townsville, Australia, in 1945.

on board the submarine, including the submarine commander, knew and fully understood what they had to do. The operational plan for the insertion of the party into Japanese-occupied Balikpapan was:

1. Night of 20-21 March — a reconniassance party comprising Stott and McMillan (Folboat No. 1), Dooland and Horrocks (Folboat No. 2) was to reconnoitre the insertion landing area, keep a low profile during the hours of daylight, then return to the submarine on the night of 22 March. If possible, it was to make radio contact with the party still at sea. Failing this, it was to try again the following night. The men in the folboats were to keep in contact with each other while at sea by means of high-frequency walkie-talkies.
2. On the night of 22 March the *Perch* was to return to the dropping zone, and await the return of the reconnaissance party. It was to remain at the rendezvous until 0100 hours. If no contact was made with the men it was to retire seawards for safety.
3. The night of 23 March. In the event of failure of the reconnaissance party by 2200 hours to return to the dropping zone, Captain Morton was to lead a second party into a new location 11 km south of Cape Tambangongot, and a few kilometres from the original insertion location.

Now, as the time approached for the reconnaissance party to leave the submarine, they assembled their folboats on the deck, and at 2200 hours launched these boats into the choppy sea. Thunder clouds growled in an angry sky. Horrocks and Dooland were first away in their folboats, but Stott and McMillan's outboard failed to start. After three attempts, Stott gave the order to commence paddling. A storm was now raging and the waves were swamping the men in their light boats. The conditions were so severe that Bill Horrocks thought the operation would be aborted, but on hearing Stott telling them to proceed on to the shore, he had no choice but to keep paddling.

He looked back at the submarine and was just in time to see it submerging beneath the windswept and choppy waters of the bay. When they were halfway to the shore, Stott suddenly noticed lights dotted around the shore area. They had to be Japanese. He knew they had no choice other than to push ahead, and hope they would not be seen. Maybe in this stormy weather they would stand more of a chance of survival against the Japanese. He was thankful that Bob wasn't with them, but was safe on the submarine.

Soaking wet, Stott grabbed his walkie-talkie: 'Enemy in sight!' he shouted over the noise of the storm. 'Go for your lives!'

Horrocks heard Stott's voice over the walkie-talkie. They had to get away from the area where the Japanese were. He shouted to Dooland: 'We've got to change course!'

Struggling with the paddles, the two men headed down the bay. Horrocks glanced behind him to see if Stott and McMillan were in sight but suddenly an enormous wave landed on them with such force that it nearly overturned the boat.

Stott and McMillan were never sighted again. On that day New Zealand lost one of its bravest heroes, a man who, perhaps, had come to the end of his nine lives after cheating death so many times. He had crammed more into his 30 years than most people would in two lifetimes.

> 'Mother, should my friends come, should my brothers come,
> Do not tell them I am dead, for they will weep.
> But spread the table, give them food and wine,
> Spread the table, let my brothers sing.'
>
> CRETAN FOLKSONG

Major Don Stott, DSO and Bar.

PART 2

Written with the generous assistance of

Frank Wigzell

INTRODUCTION

The role of SOE in the south-west Pacific area differed vastly from that of Greece and other European theatres of war. When Pearl Harbour fell to the Japanese in December 1941 it was clear that there would soon be a need for an intelligence network in the Pacific. The later falls of Malaya, Singapore, Hong Kong and Burma reinforced this view, and did very little to promote any feeling of confidence in the British military system. Therefore a British clandestine force, before it could operate successfully in the south-west Pacific, had to overcome a certain amount of scepticism.

There was also very little information on the territories occupied by the Japanese, and some of these territories were unmapped. SOE in Europe, on the other hand, had a wealth of intelligence available. These were some of the problems that SOE in the Pacific had to overcome.

There were several names by which SOE in the Pacific was known. The most common was the Services Reconnaissance Department (SRD) Force 136, and 'Z' Special Unit. In Part Two I have concentrated on 'Z' Special Unit.

The first chapter of Part Two, Chapter 5, explains what happened to the men of that ill-fated mission, Robin 1. These facts have never been published before.

'Z' Special Unit obtained most of its recruits from Australia, and to a lesser extent, New Zealand, with several more from Britain and its other colonies. This book deals largely with the New Zealand members of 'Z'. I have included the chapter on Operation Jaywick as it was one of the first major operations of 'Z', and shows the exceptional capabilities and endurance that the men of 'Z' possessed. You will read about Major Ivan Lyon, Commanding Officer of the now famous *Krait* raid on Singapore Harbour, and the ill-fated and tragic 'Rimau' operation in the following year.

Chapters 8-12 tell the story of Frank Wigzell and the other New Zealanders of 'Z' Special Unit who fought in the jungles and swamps of British North Borneo (now known as Sabah). The author gratefully acknowledges the assistance of Frank Wigzell and Lt Colonel G. B. (Jumbo) Courtney for their help and advice in the writing of the following chapters.

CHAPTER 5

Survive or Die

*'Just have one more try, it's dead easy to die.
It's the keeping on living that's hard.'*

SOURCE UNKNOWN

On the night of 21 March the USS *Perch* tried to establish contact with the four men of the reconnaissance party of Robin 1. This was not achieved, so the *Perch* tried again the following night. This also failed, and the submarine remained at the rendezvous until 0100 hours. Again on the night of 23 March no signals were received from the party.

A report by Sergeant Bill Horrocks states:

Our motor started, but the other motor didn't and Major Stott gave orders to paddle . . . in the event of our getting separated, we were to make contact by walkie-talkie. Shortly afterwards we were separated but were unable to contact boat No. 1 or the submarine. We persevered with our course and when about 400 yards from shore we grounded. At 0130 hours we heard a Japanese voice (muffled) on the walkie-talkie; at 0145 hours we heard two English voices loud and clear checking frequency. It was 0200 when we grounded and went ashore.

Horrocks and Dooland approached the shore silently, and with stooped figures did a quick reconnaissance of the beach. They then carried the folboat ashore and into the concealment of the thick tropical jungle, close to the shore line. So far so good. They tried again to make contact with Don Stott, but still no luck. That day they kept under cover, searching for Stott and McMillan. They could find no sign of them anywhere, and they had to wait until the appointed time before contacting the submarine at 2200 hours. No response. They tried again the following night with no success.

For the next four weeks Horrocks and Dooland were on the run continually from the Japanese. However, they were befriended by several local natives who provided them with what little food was available. The Japanese had requisitioned most of the food for their troops in the area.

The *Perch* had returned to the dropping zone in the bay on the night of 21 March. It had waited until the required time for the return of the reconnaissance party at 0100 hours, then returned to sea. On the night of the 22nd it again approached the dropping zone during darkness for the third time. This time the night was clear, the sea was like glass and there was good visibility.

The leader of the second party, Lieutenant Bob Morton, and the remainder of the party under his control, assembled their folboats, rubber boats and stores in readiness to disembark at the dropping zone. Suddenly, Commander Hills, who was stationed on the observation platform, noticed a strange buoy near the dropping zone, and called the Intelligence Officer of the party.

Forty years later Bill Dwyer remembers:

> We were idling by with the decks just above the surface, in order to keep a low profile, and Bob Morton decided the plan was go, as he had arranged with Stott. The word was quietly passed along the deck for me to come up on the bridge.
>
> 'What do you make of this?' said Blish Hills. 'That buoy is moving. What do you make of it, Bill?'
>
> I suggested it was probably an oil barge of the submersible type, perhaps a Japanese oil lighter.

The reaction to this was an immediate 'Destroy contact'. The third round of the main gun was a direct hit. This was followed up with about five rounds from the Bofors gun, and an oil fire started to spread across the horizon. There was now a serious danger of the main party being silhouetted against the flames, and being seen on their way in by the Japanese on the shore, and it was only after a conference with the submarine commander that the second party decided to land.

The encounter with the oil lighter was witnessed by Horrocks and Dooland who were concealed in the jungle. Bob Morton and his party left the submarine at 2230 hours, and during the journey to the shore the outboard motors failed, though they picked up closer in. They landed at 0100 hours at a point about 55 km north-east of Balikpapan, after pulling their boats through the shallow waters for the last 150 m.

At daybreak on 23 March Lieutenants Morton and Dwyer carried out a reconnaissance of the area, and found that it would be necessary to move the stores to a safer hiding place, as they were very close to a native track. The party then moved the stores as quickly as possible, watched by an inquisitive child. The child called its parents, and fortunately for the operatives, when a number of natives arrived they proved to be friendly. A quantity of food and cigarettes were given to them, and they offered to carry the stores to another place. They employed the natives as bearers, and the party moved with its equipment about 5 km inland, near a house belonging to a man named Hassan, where, after a meal provided by him, they slept in the jungle nearby.

Bill Dwyer recalls that Hassan

> was a fluent Dutch speaker and took an instant dislike to Sergeant Dey. Hassan did not like the Japanese, but he hated the Dutch even more. He had been a pilot in the Dutch Samarinda-Balikpapan service. He was known as 'Kiai' or learned one, of the area, so was much respected by the natives.

Early on the 24th, Hassan awoke the party and guided them to a new hideout a short distance further inland. The men tried to communicate with Darwin, but this failed, as the batteries failed to function. By this time, Morton was very worried about the welfare of his friend Don Stott and searched continuously for him and the other three men, McMillan, Dooland and Horrocks, but without success.

On 25 March Dwyer had made a lone reconnaissance some 5 km to the south and had established friendly relations with an old native hermit who agreed to warn the party of any Japanese movement from that direction. But the following day a native brought the news that the Japanese had seen the sinking of the oil lighter, and had come to investigate the area. They had located the main hideout for the stores, which was now under heavy guard, and an enemy patrol was moving in the direction of the Robin 1 camp. It was decided to move to a new hideout and most of the remaining stores were carried by the entire party to an intermediate place.

From post-war Indonesian sources it has been learned that the shifting of the stores from the beach on 23 March had been observed by a local native informer, Abdul Rahman, who was in the pay of the Japanese. He had made his way secretly to Balikpapan and reported the matter to the Kempei Tai,

The Robin 1 party before it left for Borneo. Back: Condoy Satu NEI, Condoy Dua NEI, Sgt Dey NEI, WO2 Farquharson AIF, Sgt Houghton NZEF, Sgt Horrocks NZEF. Front: Lt Dwyer AIF, Lt Morton NZEF, Major Stott NZEF, Capt. McMillan NZEF. (Missing Sgt Dooland AIF, Sgt Bin Ali Sali.)

who despatched a company of troops to patrol the area. They had no trouble finding the stores as the natives had pilfered many of the supplies, and discarded the empty remains and rubbish in the jungle.

Morton and Dwyer now went off to reconnoitre a new hideout, while Warrant Officer Farquharson and Sergeant Dey left to pick up Kondoy Dua (the lookout). Warrant Officer Houghton and Kondoy Satu set out to remove the remainder of the stores and make a final clearing of the old camp site. Houghton did not return from this sortie, and post-war investigation by New Zealander Lieutenant Tapper reveals that he had escaped from a Japanese patrol only to be later captured and eventually shot.

During the reconnaissance Morton's party heard shots first at short range, and then Dey returned with the news that he had been unable to find Kondoy Dua, but had run into some Japanese on the crest of a nearby hill. Shots had been exchanged and Farquharson did not return to the others. It was impossible to estimate the number of Japanese surrounding them.

A short, sharp battle ensued with Dwyer acting as rear-guard, and

Bob Morton at the training camp before departure.

fortunately there were no casualties. Morton and his men retreated into the jungle, and towards evening emerged, and went off to reconnoitre the stores hideout. This was safe and the men were able to take as much as they could carry, which included personal necessities and 4½ tins of rations. These rations proved to be very satisfactory; four men were able to live on them for two weeks. They had to leave their radio and steam generator behind as they were too heavy to carry.

The party now consisted of three operatives — Morton, Dwyer, and Dey. The four members of the original reconnaissance team — Stott, McMillan, Horrocks, and Dooland — were missing, as well as Farquharson, Houghton, and the two Kondoys. Morton and Dwyer tried continuously to locate them all, but with the active presence of the Japanese all around them being supported by native informers, they could not do much.

On 28 March, Dwyer made further reconnaissances and found Kondoy Dua, who was suffering from shock and exposure. They also located the old native hermit who had helped them before. Now he gave them the news that Farquharson had been wounded in his upper left arm and had been taken prisoner by the Japanese.

The following day Morton, Dwyer and Sergeant Dey continued to search for the lost members of their party, but long-range patrols were impossible owing to the shortage of food. They eventually found Kondoy Satu, who was also suffering from shock and exposure. He had been captured by the Japanese but his native friends had cut his bonds. However, he was in poor health, and also suffering from recurrent malaria. From him the party learned of the capture of Warrant Officer Houghton. The Malay interpreter, Bin Ali, now reappeared with several friendly natives, and appeared to be in good shape.

During the period from 29 March–17 April, the party withdrew further into the jungle for concealment, and kept a low profile. Bill Dwyer remembers:

> On 17 April, the anticipated Japanese search began, and a very rowdy force of some 100 Nips and natives came down from the north; they made such a bloody row that anyone for miles would have known of their presence. They seemed unwilling to come into the jungle in small parties. I inspected one of their rest sites after they had left, and it was a pigsty. However, it was a boost to our morale to think that they would send so many troops, and not send small parties. Perhaps they thought we were a bigger force. I have always thought that their native guides deliberately misled them as to our whereabouts.

Their only contact with the outside world was an American miniature communications receiver, on which they could obtain some international news. It was used only on rare occasions so as to conserve the battery. Boredom was a problem, and they had nothing to read, though the two officers made a chess set and a rough pack of cards with which to pass the time. Rainstorms were frequent and they all were attacked by mosquitoes, leeches and ticks.

The effective network of native intelligence now provided the good news that Horrocks and Dooland of the first reconnaissance party were alive and well. They had been adopted by loyal natives, and were some distance away. They could not rejoin the main party because of the Japanese force situated

Local perahus from the area where the party purchased their sea-going perahu for their escape.

in the jungle between them. They would have to await an opportunity, using native trackers, to return to the other party.

The men were continually hungry, and their rations were getting lighter, but Bin Ali now came to the rescue. He managed to purchase rice, yams, coconuts, fruit, shellfish, birds eggs, chicken, and on one occasion, a green turtle. The old native hermit was also supplying them with a little rice.

The supply of food came to an abrupt end when the Japanese placed a patrol around the various supply areas. Dwyer has written:

> I had grown to look forward to my daily dose of yam — it was very starchy, but it filled a gap and had plenty of fibre. We started to compete with the wild pigs for a red berry that grew on some native trees through the rain forest. We tried it on our forearms then under the arms, and on the skin inside our mouths. It had a nasty taste, but we figured that if the wild pigs lived on it, we probably could too. Apart from loose stools, there was little effect. The pigs could reach up to a height of about one-and-a-half metres and we were able to clean up the rest.
>
> We were all losing weight, and finding most patrols a heavy task. Then the patrol around the hermit man was taken away, and we were able to get about two cups of rice and some yams each week. This was a real feast. The rations had long gone, but we kept the tins for cooking gear — in fact they were a godsend as they were used for everything.
>
> In approximately six weeks from landing to escape I lost 28 kg in weight. We patrolled every day, and on one occasion, when I was out on my own, I had the fear of God put into me. I heard a noise that sounded like the Spirit of Progress hurtling down the permanent way. I rolled into defensive cover, and the sound kept on coming louder, and I was right in the way. Overhead passed about 300 monkeys and it took me many minutes to recover.

For some reason, the Japanese now withdrew all forces except the local observers from the area. Perhaps they thought that the party had ventured further into the unknown area of the interior. This news was now most welcome from the native intelligence, for Bin Ali could roam the area in search of food. Reconnaissance aircraft, sent out in accordance with the emergency plan, were seen by the men, but could not be signalled as the Japanese had surrounded them.

On 20 April Dooland and Horrocks finally joined the main party, having taken four weeks to get through the Japanese cordon with the help of native

The party escapes to sea in the perahu they bought for 1,400 guilders.

sympathisers, and one other who accompanied them. They were not in very good shape, but had managed to collect valuable information.

It was decided that the only possible course of action was to steal a native perahu and escape with this information, taking along the native informants. However, most of the perahus in the area had been either taken over by the Japanese or left broken and holed. One of the native helpers, Oesop, negotiated for several days before he was able to procure one for 1400 guilders.

Meanwhile Hassan had been contacted by Bin Ali, who told them he had been accused of helping them after the last attack on the main party. He had been taken to Balikpapan and interrogated by the Kempei Tai. The Japanese beat him severely but he did not disclose his association with the operatives, and finally escaped. He told Morton that McMillan and Farquharson were in jail, but this later proved to be incorrect.

On 29 April the men moved down to the coast and the local natives supplied them with adequate food for their voyage, with cooked rice in nipa leaf packets, coconuts, and live chickens. They also gave them a farewell feast, which played havoc with their stomachs but was good for their morale. Six of the most intelligent natives were chosen to accompany the men on their voyage back to Morotai.

On 1 May they set out in the perahu in the evening. The perahu was about 5 m long, with a beam of about 2 m. They left from a point approximately 50 km north-east of Balikpapan, and headed due east. It was imperative that they get over the horizon before first light, so they had to row as hard as they could, with the bulk of the work falling on Morton and Dwyer as the other white men were unfit and the natives unwilling.

Morton found it particularly upsetting that he had not found his great friend, Stott. It was also worrying that they had left the other operatives behind, some of whom were prisoners of the Japanese.

The second of May dawned sunny and calm, with very little breeze. At 1100 hours two B24 Liberators were sighted, but as they were far off the men were unable to attract the aircrafts' attention. The perahu continued on a north-eastern course for the remainder of that day. In the middle of the afternoon on 3 May a low-flying aeroplane was spotted about 30 km away. This time Dwyer flashed a mirror which had been taken from his escape kit, and a few minutes later a PBY Catalina flying boat landed near the perahu on the smooth surface of the water. The Catalina was a naval search and rescue aircraft from the 13th Air Sea Rescue Squadron of the US Navy, piloted by a Captain Humphries. Humphries was greeted with shouts of welcome and relief.

Machine-gune fire from the Catalina now sank the perahu, and then a course was set for Morotai. On the trip back they landed to pick up the crew of a Liberator from a beach on the west side of the Celebes Sea. With the extra load the aircraft had great difficulty in becoming airborne, having to taxi for some 15 minutes on the water. It was some time after nightfall that they landed at Morotai, and in the middle of a Japanese bombing attack, but there were no casualties.

'We're back safely,' thought Bob Morton. 'If only the same could be said for Don, everything would be perfect again . . .'

Dwyer and Morton enjoy a cup of tea on their return to base at Morotai by Catalina flying boat.

CHAPTER 6

Operation Jaywick

'Japanese troops, well armed and disciplined, invade the British colony of Malaya. Their ultimate aim — the "impregnable" fortress of Singapore, symbol of Britain's might in the East.'

DAILY EXPRESS

The first major operation of 'Z' Special Unit was Operation Jaywick, and it is necessary in this chapter to explain the importance of this raid. Operation Jaywick was one of the most audacious and successful commando raids of the Second World War. It took place on the island of Singapore.

Ronald McKie wrote an enthralling book on the raid, titled *The Heroes*. He described the commando attack as the 'greatest sea raid of the Second World War — a raid extraordinary in a war which spawned so many examples of brave eccentric virtuosity'. Launched from secret bases in Australia across 3 000 km of enemy-occupied water, a small band of commandos from 'Z' Special Unit wreaked havoc amongst shipping in Japanese-held Singapore.

To Britain, Singapore had been an impregnable fortress. Its guns faced out to sea in the event of an attack. However, the tragedy of the fall of Singapore lay in Britain's defence thinking, which ignored the fact that Singapore was vulnerable to attack from the rear — the Malayan mainland. The Japanese, who were aware of this, based their whole campaign and final assault on this failure in British military thinking.

It was little wonder, then, that in the last days of January 1942, Japanese troops on bicycles, and some on foot, attacked Singapore across the narrow Johore Strait which separated Singapore Island from the Malayan mainland, encountering no opposition.

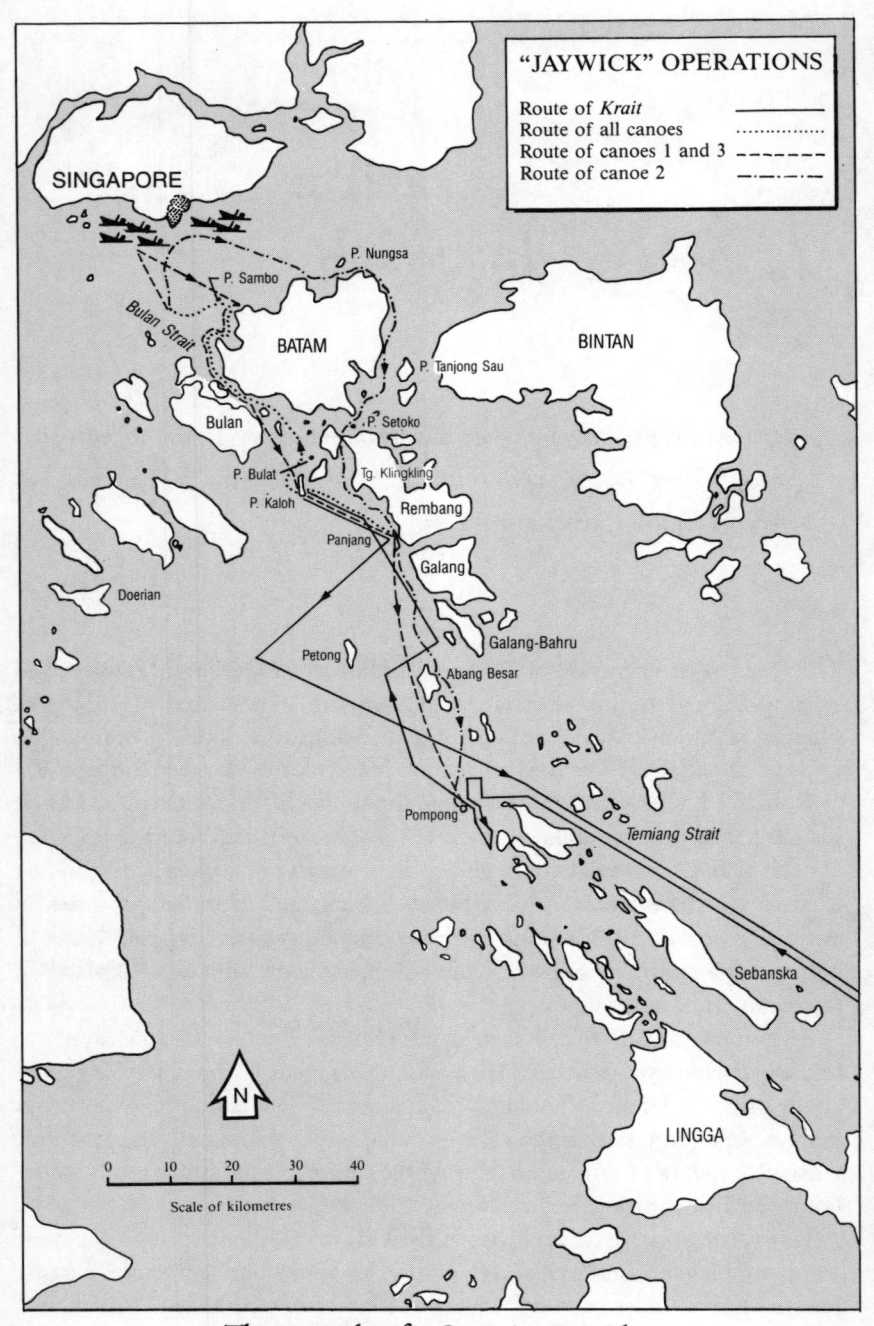

The route taken for Operation Jaywick.

Operation Jaywick was the brainchild of Captain Ivan Lyon of the Gordon Highlanders. Lyon, a 28-year-old Intelligence Officer at Army Headquarters in Singapore, had been Liaison Officer with the Dutch before being sent to Sumatra to help organise and supply an escape route for refugees across the island, and onward to safety in Ceylon and Australia. This was known as the 'Tourist Route'. Lyon subsequently was awarded the MBE for his work in Sumatra.

Lyon's plan for the Jaywick mission originated in a meeting with an Australian, Bill Reynolds, who had been given command of a fishing boat, the *Kofuku Maru*. This was operated by a Japanese firm in Singapore. When Singapore finally fell to the Japanese on 15 February 1942, Reynolds sailed the *Kofuku Maru* to the Thousand Islands of the Rhio Archipelago, and there met Captain Lyon. Lyon immediately saw the boat could be requisitioned for returning to Singapore, and started to formulate a plan, incorporating the *Kofuku Maru*.

He changed the boat's name to the *Krait*, after the deadly Asian snake of the same name. This was the beginning of Operation Jaywick. Lyon was joined by Major Campbell, Administration Officer for the expedition, while personnel for the Jaywick party were selected in Australia. On 15 August 1943 a four-months' training programme commenced at a special camp — 'Camp Z' — at Broken Bay, north of Sydney.

The men chosen for Jaywick were Australians and Britons. They underwent a body-punishing course designed to weed out those physically and mentally unsuitable. 'Z' training was not for the squeamish. It was simply a case of kill or be killed, which the commandos learned to accept as second nature.

They learned how to kill with hand, cord, knife, jungle parang or blackjack. They were taught how to use a compass, read maps and charts, find their way by day or night on land or water, move silently, camouflage themselves and their equipment, stalk an enemy sentry, climb cliffs, and go without food or water for long periods.

As one volunteer wrote afterwards:

> We trained about 18 hours a day for four months. We trained in strict secrecy, with no smokes, no beer, no women, no nothing. It was hell — the kind of life you look back on when you're very old, and want to impress your grandchildren.

When Lyon learned that his wife, Gabrielle, and small son, Clive, had become prisoners of the Japanese and were in Changi Prison in Singapore, he had an added incentive to put Jaywick into action. He had a fanaticism for the mission, a personal ruthlessness, and there was a nervous tension about him. Physically, Lyon was slight and dark, with piercing black eyes. He was a loner, was never still, slept little and ate less. To the men around him he appeared reserved and unemotional. Despite his distant, impersonal attitude and his habit of silence, he was able to convey to his men a feeling of confidence.

Lt Ted Carse, skipper of the *Krait*, describes in *The Heroes* that he

> felt a force beyond Lyon's control was driving him, compelling him towards Singapore, and that nothing the men could do would prevent this inexorable movement; and then a stray idea came to him, and in this fleeting moment he felt that the whole operation had been planned long ago, in the distant past, and that whatever was to happen, even their deaths, had already been decided.

In the beginning there was some opposition to Jaywick among the allied 'brass hats', but soon Lyon, now promoted to Major, gained the support of some influential men — Lord Gowrie, the Governor-General of Australia, Admiral Sir Guy Royle, the First Naval Member, and General Sir Thomas Blamey, the Chief of the Australian Army.

The **Krait.**

*Two crew members training in New South Wales for Operation Jaywick. The **Krait** is in the background.*

The plan for Jaywick was to use the *Krait* as a fishing boat to carry the commandos within striking distance of Singapore. When the *Krait* reached the surrounding islands of Singapore, it would go into hiding while the raiding party infiltrated Singapore's Keppel Harbour by kayak. The raiders would attach limpet mines to the shipping in the harbour and then retreat as quickly as possible.

Back in Garden Island, Western Australia, the men had received detailed instruction at Careening Bay, a special boat school. The school was concerned primarily with small submarines; the newest of these was the motor submersible canoe, known as the MSC, which was a steel canoe driven by a small electric motor. The offensive weapon of the MSC was the limpet — a 3 kg charge held by magnets to the side of the target. (Forty years later the limpets were to be used by the French to attack the Greenpeace vessel *Rainbow Warrior* in Auckland's Waitemata Harbour.) The limpets were sufficient to sink two 10 000-tonne ships if placed correctly.

The plan was an audacious and dangerous one, in effect a suicide mission, as the chances of discovery were high and the men knew that the Japanese would show no mercy if they were caught.

On 9 August 1943 the *Krait* with 14 crew on board began the 3 800 km journey from North Queensland to Exmouth Gulf, on the coast of Western Australia — the launching-point of Operation Jaywick. The 14 men, 4 soldiers and 10 sailors, were:

Major Ivan Lyon
Lieutenant D. M. N. Davidson
Lieutenant R. C. Page
Lieutenant H. E. Carse
Leading Stoker J. P. McDowell
Leading Telegraphist H. S. Young
Acting Leading Seaman K. P. Cain
Acting Able Seaman A. M. W. Jones
Acting Able Seaman W. G. Falls
Acting Able Seaman A. W. Huston
Acting Able Seaman F. W. Marsh
Acting Able Seaman M. M. Berryman
Corporal R. G. Morris
Corporal A. Crilley

The outward appearance of the *Krait* was that of a normal Japanese fishing craft. It was a wooden vessel, about 22 m long, with a final maximum speed of about 6½ knots and a range of 12 800 km.

Serious engine trouble delayed the departure of the *Krait* from Australia, and it was not until 2 September that they sailed from Exmouth Gulf, bound for the South China Sea through the treacherous Lombok Strait. To heighten its disguise, the *Krait* flew the Japanese flag from its mast and the men dyed their bodies and dressed as natives.

The vessel carried flour, rice, prunes, mainly tinned vegetables, fruit and fruit juices, tinned bully beef and finely powdered dehydrated mutton. The medical stores contained vitamins, atebrin, quinine, acriflavine, Epsom salts, and a first-aid kit. There were also some 50 000 cigarettes — English Capstans and American Camels — most of them intended as 'trade' goods or bribes for natives who might help them among the islands. Arms, ammunition and explosives were some of the heavier and bulkier items. The *Krait* carried 2 Lewis guns, 2 Brens, 8 Stens, 8 Owens and 14 Smith and Wesson revolvers, in addition to 200 hand grenades, stabbing knives, 20-cm stilettos, and jungle parangs. There were 45 limpets, enough to sink 15 ships, and 330 kg of plastic explosives.

Major Lyon, the leader of the party, was a professional soldier with experience in small boats. Before the war he had spent some time sailing around Jaywick Sands on the Essex coast with his wife Gabrielle, and so the expedition was named Operation Jaywick. However, he had no deep-sea or navigational experience. Carse and McDowell were the only two men capable of sailing the *Krait* to Singapore and back again.

Leading Telegraphist Horace Young kept a diary of his journey on the *Krait*, and the following is an extract dated 8 September 1943:

> Sighted our first objective about 21 miles — Mt Ganung Ajung — Bali's sacred mountain, and Rinjanni on Lombok — much excitement. First glimpse enemy-held territory. Just ambling along waiting for sundown — 6 p.m. Full speed ahead. We can plainly see fires and lights from native villages. A searchlight pokes its slender beam out towards us, all hold our breaths. Relief beam does not pick us up.

The raiding party had planned to use Pompong Island as a base from which to look for a suitable hideout for the *Krait*, but they decided that the island was not suitable. After investigation, they finally dropped anchor at Pandjang Island, and all operation gear, food and water for one month were landed there. The *Krait* then sailed for Borneo, leaving behind on Pandjang the raiding party of six: three officers — Lyon, Davidson, and Page; and three ratings — Falls, Jones and Huston. They were all to rendezvous on 1 October at Pompong Island with the *Krait* and the rest of its crew.

On board the **Krait***, the men stain their bodies in preparation for the Operation Jaywick raid.*

On 19 September the six men proceeded in three canoes loaded with a week's supplies to Dongas, an island at the extreme northern end of the Rhino Archipelago, from where the attack was to be made. Dongas was approximately 11 km from Singapore's Keppel Harbour, which could easily be sighted from the island.

Each man wore over a khaki shirt a black two-piece suit of water-proofed japara silk, two pairs of black cotton socks, and black sandshoes with reinforced soles. They carried on a black webbing belt a .38 revolver and 100 rounds, a sheath knife, and a short loaded rubber hose. Inside the zippered suit pockets was a small compass and a small first-aid kit containing bandages, needles and surgical thread, powdered sulpha, and morphia bottles with needles attached. When the men were dressed, Lyon showed them cyanide capsules which he said would take effect in five seconds. He would distribute these just before the attack.

During the afternoon of 27 September a concentration of enemy shipping totalling 65 000 tonnes was assembled in the area opposite Dongas. The raiding party moved to the west to Palau Suber from where it was felt an attack could be launched more successfully. The targets were selected, each canoe being allotted an alternative target.

That night the commandos, with their faces blackened, slid stealthily into the murky waters of Singapore Harbour. The night was still and steamy, and the men, clad in their rubber suits, began to wish they had worn lighter clothing. Searchlights played over the harbour. Lyon gritted his teeth, and prayed they had not been seen. Now separated and working in pairs, they attached limpet mines to seven Japanese ships. The time-delay fuses had been activated and positioned with deadly accuracy.

As Lyon was attaching the limpet to his ship, he thought of Gabrielle and his small son in Changi Prison on the eastern side of the island. There were some 12 000 people in Changi at this stage of the war, surviving somehow amidst unspeakable brutality and horrific conditions. Lieutenant Page was thinking similar thoughts. His father, formerly Deputy Administrator of New Britain, had been captured by the Japanese at Rabaul in the Pacific and was also a prisoner.

Daylight was just starting to break when the six men landed on Dongas Island again. After 10 hours in the canoes they were exhausted, but it seemed only a short time before the noise of explosions sounded across the strait. Seven explosions in all were heard, indicating that all but two of the attacks had been successful. Fifteen minutes after the first explosion, ship sirens started. Fifteen minutes later, Singapore and Sambu were blacked out.

After the first confusion, small harbour craft and motor launches patrolled the north coast of Batam Island, looking for the guerillas. After lying low for a few days the six men moved on to the rendezvous with the *Krait* as planned. On 4 October all the canoeists had been finally picked up, and the *Krait* now began its long journey back home, with its exhausted crew on board.

The following is taken from Horace Young's diary dated 11 October 1943:

Much excitement as day draws on and Lombok Island shows up. We ease down about 2 p.m. and increase as we approach strait. By 9 p.m. we were going hell for leather. Then the worst shock of the trip. About midnight each man was silently awakened to the words of a 'sail bearing down on us'. We immediately changed course and headed for Bali, about 6 miles abeam of us. Unluckily for us our 'sail' turned out to be none other than a Japanese light destroyer. She raced up and ran alongside us from about 100 yards away and our hearts stopped. Still we stood by action stations with our light machine guns feeling pretty helpless, but all determined to sell pretty dearly, seeing we were this close to home. To our amazement he turned about and slipped away towards Lombok just as rapidly as he approached. I can't describe the sighs of relief and speech that followed.

It was fortunate that the destroyer did not challenge the *Krait*, for Lyon had decided to ram the destroyer and blow up the *Krait*.

All went well for the rest of the trip and they reached Australia on 19 October 1943, the entire cruise of 6 000 km of enemy waters having been traversed without casualty or mishap. The journey to Singapore and back had taken 48 days.

On arrival in Australia, the men looked as if they were recovering from a long illness. They had lost a great deal of weight, and their faces were thin and pointed. Their dye, faded and streaked, helped to accentuate this thinness, and their eyes stretched across sunken cheeks. The mission had demanded super-human strength and courage in the face of fearful odds.

Figures later released gave Jaywick seven ships sunk or badly damaged, including the 10 000-tonne tanker *Sinkou Maru* — a total of between 36 843 and 39 111 tonnes. In addition to the material damage wrought, valuable information on port and marine conditions was brought back by the party. The secrecy of the operation was so well preserved that the Japanese attributed the attack to Chinese guerillas operating in the area.

Lyon, Davidson and Page received Distinguished Service Orders for their efforts, while Falls, Jones, McDowell and Huston received Distinguished

Service Medals. Carse, Young, Cain, Marsh and Berryman were mentioned in despatches, and Morris and Crilley each received the Military Medal.

Lt Colonel G. B. Courtney, who was Commanding Officer of Group A of the Services Reconnaissance Department in Labuan in Borneo, refers to Jaywick as an epic among small-scale raids in the tradition of Drake and Hawkins:

> Words cannot convey the anxiety these men experienced. They were under constant threat of challenge by the Japanese patrols and betrayal by local natives. Imagine the exhaustion of the canoe pairs battling against headwinds, rainstorms, and adverse tides to drive their heavily laden canoes for hour after hour through choppy seas. Jaywick was a tonic for Allied morale in the dark days of the war, a loss of face for the Japanese, and a badly needed success for SOE in India and Australia.

The *Krait* lives on. It now serves as an Australian war memorial.

CHAPTER 7

The Tragedy that was Rimau

*'Men prayed me that I set our work, the inviolate house, as a memory of you,
But for fit monument I shattered it, unfinished: and now
The little things creep out to patch themselves hovels in the marred shadow
Of your gift.'*

T. E. LAWRENCE

The story of Operation Rimau, the child of Jaywick, can now be told. I was in the middle of writing this book when the true facts of this little-known raid were made available to me. Up until then, although many of the facts had been pieced together, Rimau had largely remained a mystery.

The success of Operation Jaywick in 1943 had suggested to SOE in London that native craft could be based within the perimeter of Japanese-occupied islands for the purpose of carrying out sabotage raids, and inserting Special Operations parties into the Malayan Peninsula, Siam, and French Indo-China in support of Lord Louis Mountbatten's South East Asia Command's (SEAC) plans for invasion in 1945. To this end it was planned to carry out a repeat of Jaywick on Japanese shipping in Singapore Harbour.

The *Krait* raid was only just over when Ivan Lyon, now a Lieutenant Colonel, decided to return to Singapore. He planned a submarine-drop operation based on the use, not of canoes, as in Jaywick, but 'Sleeping Beauties'. These were electrically-powered, submersible metal boats which looked like kayaks and were known as MSCs.

Four 20-metre trawlers under construction in Australian ports were requisitioned and preparations made to alter their appearance to that of a craft similar in outline to the native junks used extensively in Singapore waters. These were referred to as 'Country Craft' and were to be powered by a 225-hp marine diesel engine, and armed with a concealed 20-millimetre Oerlikon gun.

The island of Merapas was tentatively selected as a base and plans were made to seize a junk to which stores and personnel were to be transferred from the submarine. The junk was then to be sailed to a forward rendezvous from which a co-ordinated attack by 15 midget MSC submarines could be launched against the target areas. These target areas included Keppel Harbour again, Empire Dock, and the wharves at Bukum and Sambu Islands.

Ivan Lyon had already been to England to test the highly secret Sleeping Beauties, and Rimau was intended as its first test under operational conditions. A number were brought to Western Australia for training purposes, their handling technique being difficult to master. Many trainees, using Davis underwater equipment, developed claustrophobia and had to be returned to their units.

The plan was to load 15 Sleeping Beauties aboard a Country Craft, which was being modified in a Melbourne shipyard, for the voyage to Singapore. Although folboats were to be loaded as well, to be used for escape back to a forward island base after the Sleeping Beauties had been scuttled following the attack on shipping, they were not to be used in the final assault itself. This was despite their reliability and suitability demonstrated during Jaywick the year before.

This time there were 23 men in the raiding party, led once more by Lyon, who named the operation 'Rimau' after the tiger tattooed on his own chest, which would roar when he flexed his muscles.

Ronald McKie, in his book *The Heroes*, remarks that it is significant that both Donald Davidson and Bob Page, former Jaywick operatives who were brave men willing to go on another raid with Lyon, were suspicious of Rimau. They had joined Rimau out of admiration for their friend Lyon, who was completely fearless. Page remarked: 'Ivan's crazy, but I can't let him go on his own. I can't let him down, but this raid will be my last.'

According to Lt Colonel G. B. Courtney, Commanding Officer of Group A of SRD, it was the opinion of the SRD's chief planning officer that the decision to go ahead with the raid on shipping in Singapore was taken purely for political reasons. It was to demonstrate to the Asians and the Americans that the Anglo-Australians were on the way back and to be taken seriously. In this the project had the whole-hearted support of General Blamey, Commander-in-Chief of the Australian Military Forces.

'With hindsight,' says Courtney today, 'it is difficult to justify another attack on the same target a year later, using similar methods, as it was known that the Japanese had increased their precautions in the area in the interim period. However, one must emphasise that SRD had no say in the overall decision and was told by London just to get on with the detailed planning.'

From this time onwards things began to go wrong. The shipyard workers preparing the Country Craft in Melbourne decided to go slow, then went on strike, seriously delaying the completion of the vessel. It was essential for Rimau to reach the target area by 15 October at the latest, before the change of the monsoon should make the task impossible for the next six months.

Instead, a new plan was that the whole party, with the 15 Sleeping Beauties, folboats, and all the stores, would be carried to the area by British submarine with the intention of transferring en route to a junk which was to be waylaid and captured for the final approach to the Rhio Archipelago south of Singapore.

On 11 September 1944, HM submarine *Porpoise* left Fremantle with 22 operatives, 5 British, and 17 Australians, a Royal Marine Major from SEAC and two conducting officers. This party included Lyon and four other operatives from 'Jaywick' — Davidson, Page, Falls and Huston.

As previously planned, the base was established on Merapas Island. Lieutenant W. C. Carey was left to see that the stores were safe, and plans were made to pick him up when the party returned to this base upon completion of the mission. The *Porpoise* then sailed towards the coast of Borneo to try and find a suitable junk to capture.

Junks were few and far between at this stage of the war, and the men were forced to do the best they could. They chose the *Mustika*, a type not usually seen in Singapore waters. There was no engine, but the crew taught the operatives how to manage the sails. The *Mustika* continued her voyage to a secluded and uninhabited island where the remaining members of Rimau and all stores were transferred to the junk from *Porpoise*, which then departed for Australia on 30 September, carrying the native crew of the junk for interrogation.

The members of the Rimau party had been advised that the pick-date by the submarine would be a tentative one, *Porpoise* was vulnerable to attack in clear shallow waters. It was possible another submarine would have to pick up the raiders. However, the pick-up was provisionally arranged for the night of 8–9 November, but should this not take place, Operation Rimau was to be delayed for a further 30 days, after which time the men should make their own plans to escape.

That was the last time (30 September) that SRD had any contact with the Rimau party. The whole party seemed to vanish without trace. No news came from intelligence sources of any explosions in Singapore Harbour, and there was no radio contact with any of the Rimau operatives, despite the fact that they had been equipped with two long-range radio sets.

It was not until the middle of January 1945 that a translation of an intercepted Japanese signal dated 15 October 1944 was received from United States sources, revealing that Rimau had been discovered by the Japanese, and that its members were being hunted throughout the islands. The signal arrived just in time to cause the cancellation of a rescue mission which was about to leave for the area in another British submarine.

Astonishingly, it was not until the early 1980s that most of the truth about the fate of the Rimau operatives emerged. It was only then that SRD files were released into Australian archives, and research was completed in Washington into Japanese radio-intercepted translation of parts of the war diary of the Japanese 10th Special Naval Base Unit in Singapore, and the post-war interrogation of certain Japanese naval officers. Prior to this, only Ronald McKie's book *The Heroes* gave detailed information from Japanese sources personally involved, with fragmentary investigations in the Singapore area during the immediate post-war period.

It would appear that the *Mustika* sailed towards the islands just south of Singapore, visiting the forward island base on the way, and dropping off two men as reinforcements for the conducting officer previously left there. Threading their way through the maze of islands, the Rimau men finally reached Kasu Island, about 20 km south of Singapore, undetected, but there had the misfortune to anchor within sight of a Police Coast Watching post.

The interest of the police was apparently aroused by the unusual junk, and they came out in a launch to board and inspect it. The *Mustika* opened fire, mistaking the craft for a Japanese patrol craft, and all the natives, except one, were killed. The native who was not killed managed to swim ashore undetected and give the alarm.

Ivan Lyon decided that the operation must be cancelled forthwith as he realised that the whole area would soon be swarming with Japanese. The MSC equipment was to be protected at all cost so the junk was scuttled with the MSCs inside. It was decided that men were to escape in the folboat canoes through the islands and rendezvous with the submarine at Merapas Island.

The folboats were unpacked, assembled, and stored with food and water and the junk was sunk in an unknown location. It has never been recovered. The party divided into four groups, and proceeded back to Merapas.

When the Japanese learned of the action with the native police launch they quickly alerted all the island garrisons to be on the lookout for the commandos. They caught up with the canoeists on approximately 16

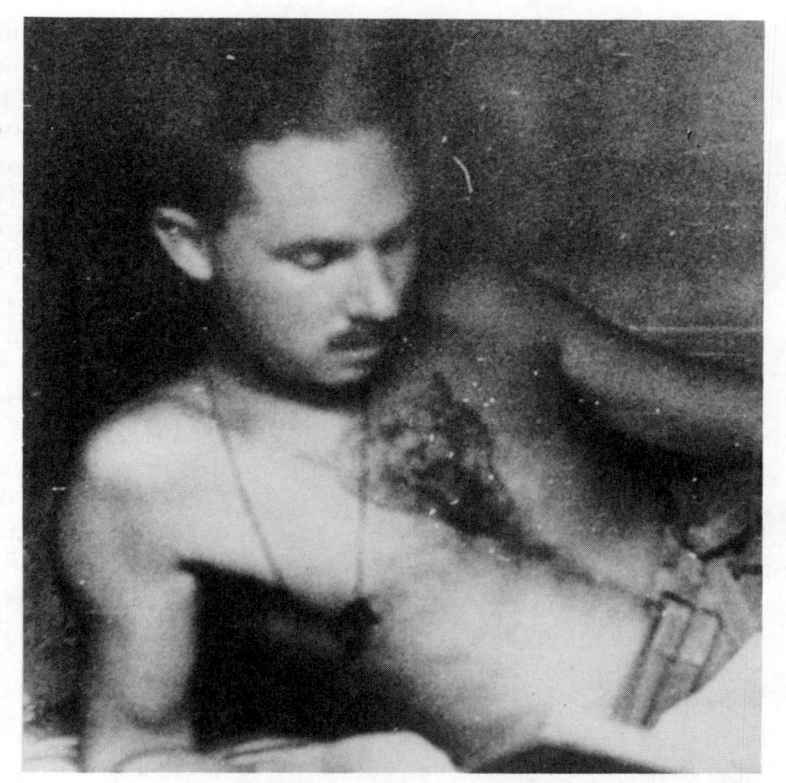

Major Ivan Lyon. Note the tiger tattooed on his chest, after which Operation Rimau was named.

October. It appears that Ivan Lyon and Davidson were killed in a skirmish with the Japanese on Soreh Island. Ross and Campbell were apparently killed on Tapai Island, five miles to the south, and it is thought that 'Happy' Houston was killed en route to Merapas.

The Japanese caught up with the party again on 4 November at Merapas, where one more member of Rimau was killed.

Unconfirmed reports relate that the remaining 18 officers and men fled to an island 8 km to the north, leaving behind a large quantity of stores, but apparently taking with them two native outrigger sailing canoes found on Merapas. Japanese evidence suggests that they waited there in the hope that the submarine would arrive on the due date, or at some time during the ensuing 30 days, and that somehow they would be able to contact her.

Subsequent movements and the confirmed dates of capture of some of the

Rimau men in the following months suggest that by the middle of November they had given up hope and were preparing to escape southwards in their canoes. At some stage before or during their flight, three men in each of the two native sailing canoes set off across the South China Sea towards the coast of Borneo, possibly to try and capture a junk in which the whole party could try to escape to Australia. By this time the north-east monsoon had set in and the native canoes are believed to have become separated on 17 December in a violent rainstorm.

A few days after, one party managed to capture a junk near the Borneo coast, but the three Australians were thrown overboard by the Chinese crew. Two of them were drowned but the third floated ashore on a log and was handed over to the Japanese by local fishermen. The other three men sailed on down the Borneo coast and through the Java Sea, leaving one of the men on an island as he was delirious with fever. The other two finally reached Romang Island off the north-east coast of Timor. It was here that they were betrayed by some natives to the Japanese, and on the 19 January 1945 they were taken to 48 Division Headquarters in Dilli, where they eventually died of wounds and neglect. The third man left on the island was eventually captured and taken to Surabaya where he is believed to have died in hospital. These men had been only a few hundred kilometres from Darwin and safety.

Meanwhile, *Porpoise* had returned to Fremantle on 11 October 1944, one day after Rimau's skirmish with the police launch. She was in need of repair, and was replaced at short notice by HM submarine *Tantalus*, which was about to leave on a routine wartime patrol in the area, east of Singapore. The Captain was briefed to the effect that, subject to patrol requirements, he should make contact with Rimau at Merapas on the nights of 8-9, and 9-10 November, and take them back to Fremantle. He was also aware that a leeway of 30 days was allowed before Rimau would finally leave the island if contact had not been made.

The *Tantalus* left Fremantle on 15 October with a Conducting Officer and an SRD Corporal who would accompany the Conducting Officer ashore if necessary. *Tantalus* arrived off the Singapore Straits on 28 October, and that night several signals were received indicating that damaged Japanese battle ships were on their way back to Singapore following the Philippines' battle. After several delays, *Tantalus* finally headed towards Merapas on 20 November.

At dawn the next day it dived and made a periscope reconnaissance of the northern end of the island, and of the rendezvous point but saw no signs of life. Just after midnight of 21-22 November the Conducting Officer and the

Corporal left *Tantalus* in a canoe to reconnoitre, and to try and establish contact with Rimau.

Tantalus returned to sea, was fired on soon after dawn by an escort vessel or destroyer, and was forced to submerge for most of the day as a Japanese seaplane was patrolling the area. It was almost as if the submarine was expected.

Meanwhile, the two men searched the island cautiously during the day and found traces of Rimau and evidence of a hurried departure some weeks before. It is known that the men had left on 4 November — four days before the first pick-up date, when the Japanese caught up with them.

During the evening of 22 November the *Tantalus* reappeared and the men in the canoe were taken aboard. From their evidence, and because of the vigorous counter-action of the Japanese anti-submarine patrol, it was decided that the risk to the submarine was too great for it to remain in the area, and it set off to return to Australia. The two nights when *Tantalus* had been cruising around Merapas had been clear, still, moonlit nights, and any Rimau survivors hiding on the island would not have failed to see it, and signalled accordingly.

On 15 and 21 October signals from the Japanese naval and military authorities in Singapore, announcing that Rimau had been discovered and was being hunted down, were intercepted by the US Communications Intelligence Services. Usually it would have taken about seven days for these signals to have been decoded, translated, and passed to the Allied Intelligence Bureau for SRD, in which case it would have been possible to order *Tantalus* by radio to hurry immediately to Merapas ahead of schedule to rescue Rimau survivors. If this had happened, they might have arrived ahead of the Japanese on 4 November, or if not, at least have discovered that Rimau had failed. But sadly for the Rimau men, these signals were not translated until some months later.

Members of 'Z' Special Unit today presume that the reason for this was that the Americans were fully occupied with urgent traffic during the invasion of the Philippines. Rimau was operating in SEAC's area, and therefore would have been of low priority in United States' eyes. It was not even mentioned in Allied Intelligence Bureau status reports to General Headquarters during that period.

From a translation of part of the war diary of the Japanese 10th Naval Special Base Unit of Singapore, it is learned that the surviving members of Rimau fled south-west in their canoes, past the islands of the Rhio Archipelago down through the Lingga Archipelago. It appears that they may have intended to rendezvous at an island which had been visited by

Jaywick the year before, where some stores had been left. Possibly they hoped to wait there for the return of the six men in the native sailing canoes with a captured junk in which they could sail back to Australia. However, by the second half of December they had evidently split up and, in separate actions through the Lingga Archipelago, one had been killed and one drowned. The remainder were captured and imprisoned in Dabo Police Station on Singkep Island.

They were later transferred to the Kempei Tai Interrogation Centre in Singapore, where they were joined in February 1945 by their companion who had been rescued from the sea, off the east coast of Borneo. In mid-February, after interrogation, they were transferred to Outram Road Jail in Singapore. One man had died in January, a few days after his arrival in Singapore, from malaria.

The remaining 10 officers and men were tried on a charge of espionage by a Japanese Army Military Court on 3 July 1945, found guilty, and sentenced to death. The court based its verdict on evidence extracted under interrogation. It is a fact that these courts were convened solely for the purpose of passing sentence. They were not trials as we understand them. Japanese intercepts in Washington archives reveal that instructions had been received from the Commander-in-Chief of 7th Area Army as early as February 1945 that the Rimau men were to be condemned to death.

In the interval between the surrender of Japan on 15 August 1945 and the arrival of British Troops in Singapore on 5 September, all records concerning the capture, interrogation, trial, and execution of the Rimau prisoners were destroyed, and even their very existence concealed. Their grave was discovered by the British authorities by accident, and the only evidence eventually obtained from the Japanese officers involved in the Military Court was concocted by those officers themselves, then in prison awaiting trial for war crimes.

On 7 July 1945, the day the prisoners were to be beheaded, a Korean prisoner watched the Rimau men move out to die. 'They all knew they were going to be executed,' he wrote. 'When they left the prison they were in high spirits, laughing and talking and shaking hands with one another. We were all amazed.'

Only Lieutenant Bob Page and Able Seaman 'Poppa' Falls had also taken part in the Jaywick raid.

A Japanese report of the execution scene says: 'The sky was clear and the scenery was beautiful . . . none said goodbye, but each man said good luck.'

CHAPTER 8

The Formation of 'Z' Special Unit

*'Round the high mountains, round the peaks swirls the air,
But earth and heroism are not found every day.'*

CRETAN RIZITIKA

To understand how the formation of 'Z' Special Unit came about, it is necessary to retrace our steps to Baker Street, London. This was the headquarters of Special Operations Executive, which was responsible for the European theatre of operations. Its secret agents were infiltrated into occupied territories, by aircraft, parachute, submarine, or fast surface craft.

The main reason for its formation was to promote resistance in countries overrun by the Nazis, and in the words of Winston Churchill 'to set Europe ablaze'. Assistance was given to resistance groups in different areas, and radio reports of intelligence were recorded and transmitted to the United Kingdom. Escape networks, sabotage and demolition played an important part in the lives of all the operatives. At the end of the war approximately 1700 specialists in undercover work had been inserted into Europe. The life of an SOE agent was, in most cases, a short one as the casualty rate was exceedingly high.

With the British war effort concentrated in Europe and North Africa, little preparation for SOE activities was undertaken in South-East Asia, and none at all in the south-west Pacific area. In July 1941, a training school had been established near Singapore, but the organisation of secret agents was actively discouraged by the civil and military authorities. This was so as not to alarm the local inhabitants by implying that their country was not impregnable and the Malayan forests not impenetrable.

This situation changed in 1942 when SOE advised the Allied Intelligence Bureau and the Australian Army, both with their headquarters in Australia, that there was a real necessity to establish a specialised force in undercover work in the south-west Pacific area. The Australian Government immediately approved of this, and operatives from SOE United Kingdom were seconded to the Allied Intelligence Bureau (AIB), to instruct in the methods approved and taught in their schools.

The need for a special-operations organisation had become even more apparent from the disastrous experiences of Malaya and other countries north of Australia. The momentous changes in the Pacific following the outbreak of war with Japan on 7 December 1941 made it imperative that a network of operations be set up behind the expanding Japanese lines. The need for a special-operations organisation based in Australia had long been apparent to the Army, Navy and Air Force authorities, but it was now an obvious necessity to harrass the enemy in every conceivable way in those territories which had already been occupied.

However, there were few people in the Pacific who had had any instruction in special operations work, or who belonged to any supporting organisation. Therefore it was necessary to introduce the bulk of the operatives into the Dutch East Indies, Malaya and elsewhere, before the Japanese had time to consolidate their positions in those areas.

In March 1942 the Rt Hon John Curtin, Prime Minister of Australia, approved the establishment of a bureau for the purpose of undertaking espionage in enemy-occupied territory, and the dissemination of propaganda amongst the native races of occupied territories. This also had the approval of General MacArthur as Allied Theatre Commander.

In June 1942 an organisation called 'Z' Special Unit was formed as the administrative unit named for Special Operations Australia. It was named by General Thomas Blamey, Commander-in-Chief of the Australian Military Forces, and named 'Z' as it was the last letter in the alphabet. Some SOE-trained British officers who had escaped from Singapore became the nucleus of 'Z'. These men, with their headquarters in Melbourne, faced a daunting task of recruiting and training officers and men from a reluctant military establishment which had no conception of the nature of special operations, and little sympathy for such an unconventional mode of warfare. To make matters worse, senior American intelligence and operational staff in the south-west Pacific area did not take kindly to an independent body of intelligence operating in an area they regarded as their own.

However, by December 1942 the Allied Intelligence Bureau had become fully operational and had assumed direct control of the Netherlands East Indies sub-section. In March 1943 the Services Reconnaissance Department (SRD) was formed. This was a security name given as a cover for Special

The 'Z' Special Unit badge and wings.

Operations Australia. The role of SRD was to train and equip agents to be infiltrated into occupied territories, to harass enemy lines of communication, general sabotage, attacks on shipping, and organising local resistance. Training schools, usually under cover names, were established to carry out instructions in SOE techniques, methods and equipment. Recruits were taught special methods of insertion and infiltration; how to operate in small parties; how to maintain communications using special equipment; and how to live in the jungle and work with the natives.

Special instruction was given in Malay, intelligence, small boat and submersible craft operation, wireless transmission, medicine, and other subjects necessary to the efficient operation of field parties. The training schools were at Cairns, Fraser Commando School in Queensland, the School of Eastern Interpreters in Melbourne, Careening Bay Camp, which was a special boat school in Perth, Camps 6 and 8, at Mt Martha, near Melbourne, Advanced Training Camp, Morotai, and Advanced Training Camp at Darwin. There were Parachute Training Units at Richmond, New South Wales, and Leybourn, in Queensland. There was a Signals Training Centre at Bonegilla, and a School of Military Engineering at Liverpool.

Fraser Island, situated off the coast of Queensland, was selected in

October 1943 as the site for the main SRD commando training school. This island had ample facilities for jungle and amphibious training, and was relatively secluded, the only other inhabitants of the island being a small forestry establishment. One hundred students at a time could be accommodated.

The training courses were revised from time to time, in keeping with the latest methods of instruction from SOE United Kingdom. The would-be operatives came from all walks of life. They included Australians, New Zealanders, British, Dutch, French Canadians, Chinese, Timorese, Malayans and Ambonese. The demanding nature of the subjects taught was such that, if any one faltered in any category, he was immediately returned to the unit from which he had been selected. Those who made it into the closed ranks of 'Z' Special Unit were tough, ruthless men, capable of killing the enemy silently and expertly.

Conditions governing special operations in the south-west Pacific area were found to be very different from those experienced in Europe, and many preconceptions had to be modified or abandoned.

In 1944 the Americans were concentrating on a direct attack against the mainland of Japan. They decided that the Australian forces could be usefully employed against by-passed Japanese garrisons in Borneo and elsewhere in preparation for the liberation of British and Dutch colonial territories to the south and east — a campaign in which the Americans did not want their own troops to become involved.

The Allied General Staff and Allied Intelligence Bureau, who were the controllers of SRD, required an efficient intelligence network of operatives in this area to provide the Australian 9th Division with accurate information relating to the strength and location of the enemy forces prior to their invasion by the Australians in June 1945.

Out of this was born the Semut operation, aptly named as 'semut' in Malay means 'ant', and its operatives, like ants, would have to go to ground. Operation Semut was placed on the priority list for entry into occupied Borneo.

The Allies controlled Morotai Island, which is off the north-east tip of New Guinea. Borneo could be penetrated by long-range aircraft. The B24 Liberator was the best aircraft for such a mission, as it could attack shipping and ground targets because of its ability to remain in flight for a considerable period. Economical on fuel and with a great carrying capacity for supplies and bombs, it was easily adapted for the dropping of parachutists and supplies into occupied territories. Submarine entry on the coastline was considered a bad risk as the coastal Malay were unreliable, frequently taking bribes from the Japanese. The Japanese controlled the coastal regions, but not the interior of Borneo.

Operation Semut was to consist of two parts. Firstly, there was to be a reconnaissance mission of eight operatives under the command of Major Tom Harrisson, a former member of the King's Royal Riflemen and the Green Howards. Harrisson had been stationed in Northern Ireland and was seconded to 'Z' through SOE in Britain. In 1932 he had led Oxford and Cambridge University parties into Borneo on an anthropology study. He seemed a logical choice for Borneo.

Major Toby Carter, a New Zealander who was in Australia with his wife and daughter when the Japanese entered the war, and who had been inducted into the Australian Army, was to be operational Commander, and parachute into Borneo with the second group of operatives. Carter had been a surveyor with Shell Oil at Brunei before the war.

Major Harrisson, operating from the Morotai base, and flying with the US Navy and Flight 200 RAAF Liberators (B24s) flew four missions into Borneo in the Sarawak area before finally finding a suitable area for the insertion of the advance party.

A cleared area on the Kelabit Plateau, approximately 1700 m above sea level in the mountainous Tamabo region, and known as the Plains of Bah, was agreed on for the drop. This was an unknown and previously unmapped area of Sarawak.

The advance party was immediately despatched and, after two aborted flights in the early mornings of 23-24 March, the third, on 25 March 1945, was successful. The party of four from the first Liberator, including Major Harrisson, landed in marshy scrub beside the Plains of Bah.

Sergeant Fred Sanderson, an Australian who spoke fluent Malay, was soon in contact with the native Kelabits of the area. The second drop with the remaining four operatives was safely carried out. They were 5 km off course, but arrived four hours later at the longhouse to find Harrisson being entertained by the head man, Lawai Bisarai, of the Bario Kelabit tribe. Rice

One of the RAAF B24 Liberators used for parachute and supply dropping.

wine, or borak as it was known, flowed freely.

Contact was made with Darwin by Boston radio using a hand generator but Darwin was unable to decode the cipher messages sent by the reconnaissance party. Headquarters interpreted the message to mean that the party had been compromised by the enemy — that is, that they had been captured by the Japanese, and someone had informed the enemy enabling them to use the operatives' wireless and code.

Major Carter disbelieved this story and advised headquarters that the operation would proceed. Carter's decision to go ahead proved to be the right one, and Operation Semut, with Major Carter's party of eight, was now known as Semut 2.

It was agreed after the arrival of Major Carter's party that as radio communications between the two parties could be a serious problem, the two groups would have to operate individually. Harrisson's group was named Semut 1, and Carter's Semut 2. Both Semut 1 and 2 would operate under their own leadership, and Major Carter's party immediately left for the Barum River area, south-east of Brunei.

Both groups received generous drops of materials and weaponry, much to the delight of the many indigenous chiefs who had travelled for days to meet the white men, known to them as Orang Puteh, who came from the skies. The natives pledged their loyalty and a network of security was implemented. Guerillas were issued with rifles and ammunition, and runners brought reports from the operatives who were now spreading out in all directions.

With the reconnaissance of the Bawang Valley just over the Dutch border, it was decided to move Harrisson's group to Belawit, a well-cultivated rice-growing zone in Central Borneo.

The second group of operatives were sent to various areas in British North Borneo and Sarawak. Australian Bob Long of the Semut 2 party was transferred to Semut 1 as wireless operator. Bob Griffiths, also from Australia, a railway engineer from Mildura, who had worked on the Victoria Line railway, set about draining two paddy fields and, with the help of 300 Kelabits carrying soil in head-baskets, levelled the surface for the new landing strip. Bamboos approximately 30 cm in diameter were cut, then split along their lengths, opened, then flattened out and spread over the surface of the landing strip, and pegged to the ground at each corner. With two such 5 m bamboos, a 10 m wide runway was now completed — a length of 90 m. This was then increased to 120 m and later 165 m.

High octane fuel in 4-gallon tins were dropped from a Catalina flying boat. This was to replenish the tanks of the incoming Auster aircraft, which

The Bawang Valley in Belawit, showing the bamboo landing strip.

flew from fields situated firstly in Tarakan, and then Labuan in the Bay of Brunei.

Ten days after the arrival of the second Semut 1 party, a third party of 8 operatives, which included Frank Wigzell from Auckland, New Zealand, parachuted into Belawit, making a total of 24 operatives. Of these 24 operatives, 20 were Australians, three were Britons and one was a New Zealander. In a few hours after leaving Morotai Island, the operatives had moved back in time a hundred years.

CHAPTER 9

For Special Duties

'Man's courage is the only true wealth;
Eat, drink and make the best of the world.'

CRETAN RIZITIKA

Borneo is a hot, sultry island of lush vegetation, tropical birds and many varieties of animals. It is situated in the Malay Archipelago, bounded on the east by the Sulu Sea, the Celebes Sea, and the Strait of Makassar, on the south by the Java Sea, and on the west and north by the South China Sea. It is a mountainous land, especially in the north and in the central sections, with some mountains, like Mt Kinabalu, rising to more than 4000 m.

It is a land of indigenous tribes — Kelabits, Ibans, Dayaks, Tagals, Muruts, Punans, Kayans and Kenyans. The jungle is millions of years old, with an interior so dense that few white men have penetrated it. The climate is extremely humid, especially in the coastal regions, with heavy rainfall and a monsoon season between October and May.

Animals such as elephants, rhinoceroses, several species of monkey, hornbills, orangutans, wild oxen, tiger cats, honey bears, porcupines, flying squirrels, flying foxes, red bull ants and various species of deer and pig abound. Reptiles include the crocodile, lizards and the deadly python.

This, then, is the land where Frank Wigzell and other New Zealanders fought a war, a long way from their home.

In 1939, at the outbreak of the Second World War, Francis Alexander Wigzell enlisted for overseas service and entered Trentham Military Camp near Wellington. He was 18 years of age, tall and stockily built, with sandy hair. As many other New Zealanders did at that time, he brought his age forward by two years, and when his true age was discovered he was promptly transferred to a territorial unit. This was a light armoured fighting

The young Frank Wigzell before he left New Zealand.

vehicle regiment in the Waikato area. There he attained the rank of Sergeant — Acting Squadron Sergeant-Major — and attended a specialists' course at Waiouru where he was recommended for a commission.

As the war in Europe was developing at a fast pace, Wigzell dropped rank in order to obtain an overseas posting. Early in 1942 he served with the 3rd Division Signals Headquarters in the Pacific. He saw service on the islands of Vella la Vella, Mono, Stirling, and Green Island, also known as Nissan Island.

He returned to New Zealand in August 1944, tough and fit, and was stationed at Trentham again, where the morale of the returning troops had dropped substantially, as nothing was known of their future assignments. While Wigzell was at Trentham he saw a notice on the barracks board, which stated that eight men were to be selected for a special job, and those with certain qualifications were to be interviewed immediately. Wigzell was intrigued by this and accordingly was interviewed by the reviewing officer, Major Don Stott, DSO and Bar.

'Stott was full of enthusiasm and started to interrogate me straight away on my initial training in New Zealand,' says Wigzell. 'He also asked me about the operations that I had experienced whilst on active service. He then told me that the operation was in the Pacific, and something of what it was about. I was then given a chance to withdraw. When I did not do so, I was told to have a cigarette and relax. Stott then told me about his SOE operations, including his parachuting into Greece. I became totally engrossed in what he was saying, and my confidence steadily grew in this man. I came to the conclusion that he was a leader whom one could rely upon and trust implicitly. Stott told me his motto was "check and double-check" which I was to learn later was a life-saver when put into operation.'

Wigzell knew that he would not have been given the above information if he had not been accepted into the group. Ten days' special leave was granted, and when they returned to camp, the selected eight men, including two infantry officers, boarded the USS Co. freighter *Waipouri* — a small cargo vessel of about 5000 tonnes — for Australia.

'What an experience,' says Wigzell. 'We stood to at dawn and dusk, and there were several unexplained sightings reported, but finally we arrived at our destination — Melbourne.'

Leave was granted over the Christmas holidays, and the group was entertained at a special New Zealand night organised by the High Commissioner in Melbourne. Later, the New Zealanders met for the first time their new Australian partners for their future theatre of operations — Borneo.

Early in the New Year the party was told to go north and report to the commando and guerilla training camp on Fraser Island, north of Brisbane. The first part of the journey was by rail, but the men were then transferred to a cattle truck, the floor of which was covered with straw. The men stretched their legs and slept in comfort.

When they arrived in Brisbane, Wigzell, together with George Edlin from Invercargill, New Zealand, noticed a brewery named 'Bulimba'. Broke and feeling very thirsty, they decided to try and obtain a beer at a reasonable cost. They approached the manager's office, introduced themselves, and told a story about how, as Kiwis, they were interested in the Australian methods of brewing. They would appreciate it if they were permitted to view the brewery.

The manager was a New Zealander and he arranged for them to be given a complete inspection of the brewery by one of the foremen. After they had been shown around they were told to wait until everybody had finished for the day. At knock-off time a hogshead appeared on the landing bay. To Wigzell's and Edlin's surprise and delight, a carload of women also arrived bringing that great Australian special, fish and chips. Tables were set up, and glasses by the dozen produced. With the arrival of the staff a lively party was soon under way, which continued late into the night. It was two worn-out Kiwis who were given a fond farewell next morning. The Australians had a fair idea that something of major importance was taking place in the north.

The group of would-be commandos now finished the last part of their journey, travelling from Maryborough to Urangan, and lastly by boat to Fraser Island. They were now to gain first-hand experience of commando and guerilla warefare, for without this knowledge they would be unlikely to survive.

At Fraser Island the men learned to use folboats, which are the same as modern kayaks. The exercises at sea were in extreme conditions, and one mistake in navigation off this part of the Australian coastline could have been their last. The men then progressed to limpet mine training, and many runs were made at the shipping in the harbour. One special tactical operation was to proceed up the Maryborough River during the hours of darkness on an incoming tide, and attack the shipping and wharf areas with the limpets. On completion of this exercise, the men returned to the coast with the outgoing tide, and faced the task of an 11-km slog to Fraser Island. This was a harrowing experience, but it had its lighter moments for Wigzell. Unknown to the rest of the men taking part in the exercise, he and his partner went quietly into Maryborough for a delectable meal of fresh fish and chips.

At Fraser Island the focus was on physical fitness, with early morning runs before breakfast. These were hard and demanding. The average age of the men was 20, and they wrestled, boxed, climbed steep cliffs, learned unarmed combat, night movement, weapons and explosives. They soon learned how to kill with jungle parang, blackjack, hand, cord and stiletto. They learned how to read maps and charts, use a compass, find their way by day or night, and how to go without food and water for long periods.

Learning Malay was also an essential part of their training, and in the mess at night they were not allowed any food unless they asked for it in Malay. Their studies finished at 8 p.m. but they were expected to continue studying late into the night. Occasional leave to the mainland was permitted but the only method of transport was to team up with another operative and paddle a folboat.

One of the self-defence instructors was a top professional wrestler who thought that Kiwi Army types were fair game.

'He gave us a hard time,' says Wigzell. 'He was always shouting at us and calling us stupid bastards. I ached in all joints on one occasion, but we weren't going to let him get the better of us — we gave as good as we got.'

Explosives was to become one of Wigzell's favourite subjects, particularly the plastic variety, which was known as PE. It was easy to manipulate and could be relied upon not to explode prematurely without detonation. Almost with reverence, the operatives would clamp the detonators to the fuses with their teeth, until continual use made crimping in this fashion second nature. They were fully trained in all the different methods of detonating the explosives, including the time switch, pencil switch, pull and pressure switches. The delay and instantaneous detonating fuses made the operatives more confident.

At this stage they were not trained in jungle warfare as many of them had experienced actual combat conditions in the Pacific. This was to be taught later to them by experts in their own domain — the headhunters of Borneo.

The wireless operators were taught coding, and Wigzell was introduced to one of the best sets that he had ever operated — the Boston Mk 3 transceiver. This had a range of over 4 800 km and had superb quality and clarity of reception. The transmission did not vary as it was a crystal frequency operated set. In private life Wigzell had studied accountancy, electricity and telegraphy, and he had practised various methods of bounce and skip transmission in hilly country with good results. This knowledge would be significant when the men arrived at their eventual destination, just as it had previously been beneficial to him in the Pacific theatre of operations.

The men left Fraser Island knowing that they were now fully skilled in survival techniques. However, their training was not over yet. They had one more course to complete — parachute training, one of the means of entry into occupied countries. They were to learn this at Richmond, New South Wales. They had been there for two weeks, and were preparing for their first jump, when an urgent communiqué from advanced headquarters arrived. The majority of the men were urgently required to report to Morotai Island, as the first party into Borneo, code-named Robin 1 under the leadership of Major Don Stott, had been reported overdue, and presumed lost in action. There had been no word from Major Stott or the other 11 operatives, following their insertion by submarine into Balikpapan.

Wigzell's party was to set up a search-and-rescue operation from Morotai. This party was called Robin 2. In 1944 Borneo was an extremely difficult country to fly into, let alone parachute into. Very little was known of its interior and its climate. There were few open spaces as the jungle was dense and impenetrable. In other countries where the practice of jungle warfare and infiltration of paratroopers was carried out, the jungle was open and there was grassland and scrub. There was also a reasonable chance of intelligence information for contact and dropping, but Borneo was vastly different. The island was sparsely populated and, away from the immediate coastline, the only clearings (which show as light patches from the air) were the result of rice cultivation. These open places were a mass of tree stumps and tree trunks only partially felled within the virgin forests.

Knowing he was about to go into action, Wigzell hoped he would not have to miss out on several parachute training features but luckily he received permission to have New Zealander Frank Leckie as controller and to complete the course. On his last parachute lesson, he negotiated the first obstacle which was a 13-m tower. This tower had a direct drop on to a sandpit. The men had been taught to drop in a relaxed position in a forward or side roll. Wigzell quickly advanced to a 45 degree parachute slide and harness drop, which ended with a release at high speed still attached to the harness and into the sand pit. However, he was slow to adjust the swing, and landed slightly off centre, rolled, and hit his elbow on the side of the pit.

'Bloody hell!' shouted Leckie. 'Can't you do anything right? You'll have to do better than that.'

Feeling slightly sick, and with his elbow numb, Wigzell got up slowly from the ground, and hoped that there were no broken bones. Later he reported the injury to the Regimental Aid Post and it was rubbed with an oily linament. He was to find out many years later that the bone had been slightly splintered, and he was admitted to a private hospital in New Zealand for the removal of the pieces. Such was Wigzell's determination to join the

Robin 2 party that he kept the pain of the injury to himself, in case he was rejected for the Borneo operation. In fact, the injury caused him very little trouble while he was in Borneo, except when he transmitted for lengthy periods.

It was now May 1945. The Robin 2 party waited 24 hours on standby, then travelled north by DC3 to Darwin and then on to Morotai Island in the Halmahera group of islands. During the flight they struck a patch of 'no air' between two mountain ridges in the New Guinea area, and the plane dropped 10 000 feet before it recovered. They were lucky, for three days earlier two fighter aircraft had been lost in similar conditions.

They could see two cleared tracks in the jungle below them, and the pilot remarked that those were made by the unlucky aircraft. As they approached Morotai Strait, the RAAF radio reported that they were being followed by an unidentified aircraft, and as they were in range of the Japanese aircraft still operating in that locality they were instructed to descend to sea level. Fighter aircraft from Morotai were on the way, and if they were attacked they were to knock out their portholes and use their automatic weapons. However, no encounter with enemy aircraft occurred, and they duly arrived at Morotai.

The search and rescue operation at Balikpapan for the Robin 1 party was nearly underway when a PBY Catalina patrol plane reported picking up seven members of the lost party, plus the Malay interpreter. Wigzell's party, Robin 2, was now disbanded. As the member of the party with the longest operational service overseas, Wigzell was asked to join Major Tom Harrisson's Semut 1 party in Sarawak. Harrisson had no idea that Wigzell still had not completed the parachute-training course, and within 24 hours, having had no time to pack any clothes, Wigzell was on a B24 Liberator heading for the interior of Borneo. At last, thought Wigzell to himself, he was going on a mission.

All the men on the B24 Liberator who were parachuting into Borneo wore skull crash hats, and floppy jungle hats were tucked into their camouflaged green shirts. Some wore jungle green trousers, while others, like Wigzell, wore jungle green shorts, long socks, and green canvas lace-up boots.

The operatives had a choice of weapons. Most carried US .30 calibre Carbines, Sten or Owen sub-machine-guns, plus the usual web gear for carrying ammunition clips, and small back packs. They all carried a stiletto, 20-cm blade knife for close-contact warfare, and some had silent, single-shot pistols — the Wellrod .38. The Smith & Wesson .38 revolver was a popular choice, as was the .45 US Colt.

On entry into occupied areas the commandos carried in their back packs sufficient food, ammunition, medical supplies and money to enable them to remain in the field for a few days. On certain occasions when parachuting into action, they would wear an enlarged boiler suit, to prevent their apparatus becoming entangled with the shroud lines of the parachute. A whistle was also packed in their equipment as it would be a means of contact with other parachutists who were blown off course, and some distance from the dropping zone in the jungle.

Wigzell continues the story:

> I felt exhilarated, and there was a nervous lump in the pit of my stomach, but it all went sour in the first four hours of flight. There were eight men parachuting in, including Harrisson, so the waist gunners' compartment was now jammed with people. I was ordered to go into the bomb-bay for the duration of the flight, and as I was dressed only in shorts and jungle shirt I was shivering with the cold. Later I was taken by the Observer to the observation area, and given a hot cup of coffee and a cigarette. The Observer opened the bomb-bay doors, and on a signal from the navigator, dropped a football through the open bay and watched as it sailed down to a kampong below. I believe that this was part of Toby Carter's Semut 2 area. Just then Bill Nibbs of the Australian Infantry Forces told me that Harrisson did not know that this was my first jump, and had decided I was to be No. 4 in the first stick. I don't mind admitting I was scared as hell, and needed a bit of a boost at that moment. Bill helped me don my parachute and attach the play-line to the short static line of the B24. I heard Harrisson say 'If he doesn't jump, take him back to base'. How I detested this man's guts for saying such a thing just then, but I resolved to show him that I could jump. I had been warned at the send-off party at Morotai that Harrisson thought colonial NCOs were inferior, and accordingly should be treated as such. Later on in Borneo, other operatives confirmed this.

Harrisson was 1.81 m tall, of medium weight with a regulation short army-style hair cut, and usually wore a cap with a Major's crown. On this occasion he was despatcher, but he delayed Wigzell's jump after the green light appeared, with the result that the last two men in the stick overshot the dropping zone.

The first three men easily slid out of the aircraft through the camera hatch and down a slide. Then it was Wigzell's turn. Australian Bill Nibbs grabbed

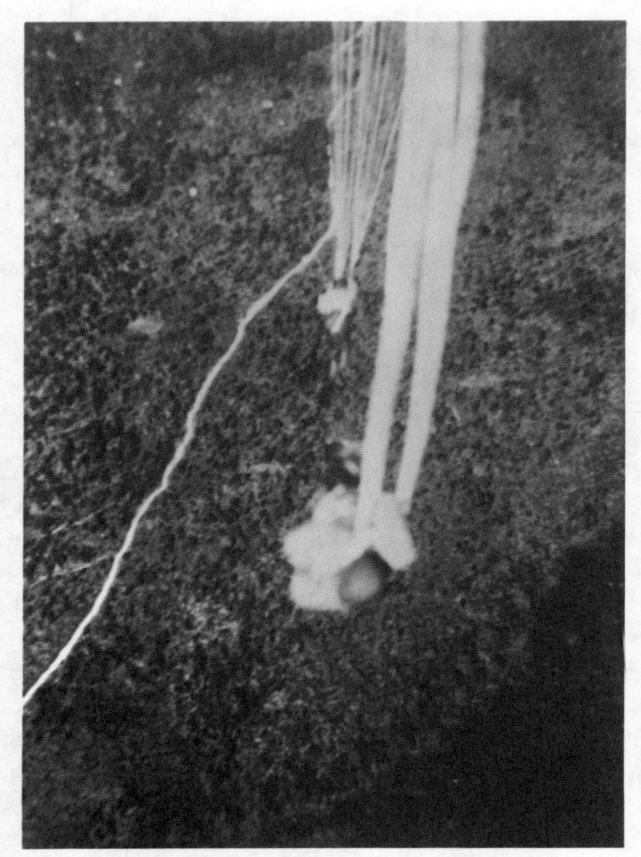

The second party of Semut 1 parachute into the Bawang Valley, Belawit.

his arm, as he was exiting too fast, held it for a second, and then hit him on his helmet. There was no time to change his mind now. He immediately shot out the hatch, and instantly came into contact with the slipstream of the aircraft at a dropping speed of 200 knots. It seemed like an eternity but it was only about a second until he felt the final pluck of the parachute from the pack and the breaking of the 13 m of play-line. Then magically the chute opened and there was suddenly dead silence all around him. He looked up and saw all the lines were untangled.

'Hell, man,' he said to himself as he floated down to earth. 'You did it.'

Euphoria turned to disillusionment in the next few moments. He was suddenly over water and as he prepared to push his release button he landed in about a foot of water in a paddy field. His parachute collapsed behind him on the surface of the water. Laughing native Kelabits from the nearby longhouses came dashing through the paddy fields, picked him up, and deposited him on to the new airstrip. This was his first sighting of the natives of Borneo.

The Kelabits were, on average, 1.68 m in height and were clothed only in loin cloths, but some had bark jackets. They smiled and talked to each other and seemed a contented lot. Wigzell immediately rewarded them with a few packets of American Old Gold cigarettes which he had concealed inside his shirt. Harrisson reprimanded Wigzell when he saw what he had done. He relieved him of the cigarettes and told him that they would be shared amongst the rest of the operatives.

'According to the rest of the operatives,' said Wigzell, 'this never happened. Never in my two-and-a-half years of operational service in action had I ever met an officer of such calibre and attitude towards his men and the natives. I was later to see further evidence of this. Such was my introduction to Semut 1.'

Wigzell's entry into Borneo had not got off to a good start with Harrisson. With his mates, he was now totally isolated from the rest of the Allied forces and totally dependent on his own actions for survival in this area. Would he make it back to the company of his friends, or would he remain forever in this environment, interred in its soil?

CHAPTER 10

Encounter with the Japanese

*'Fate — I don't fear you now,
Whatever you want to do to me,
If you have other torments I'm right here, come to me.'*

CRETAN MANTINADE

Wigzell had been the last man added to the Semut 1 party and there had been no time for him to pack any extra clothing or weapons as the storepedos had already been packed on to the plane. He therefore arrived in Belawit with what he was dressed in. Harrisson told him that he could obtain what he needed from the men who were already there, as nothing was held in reserve in the local store sulap. His instructions were to stay at the wireless sulap and assist Australian Bob Long for a few days. Bob Long was the only other wireless operator in the group. He advised Frank to have his .45 automatic cleaned and oiled as it was wet when he had landed in the paddy field.

'Give it to Ojita,' said Long. 'He will take it apart and clean it well. Leave the mag in.'

The two men went next door to a small hut where they met Ojita, a captured Japanese construction worker. When Japan had declared war, Ojita had become a conscientious objector.

'Hell,' thought Frank. 'What gives in this place?'

He did not have to worry. The pistol, plus magazine and ammunition were promptly returned, efficiently cleaned. It was just as well the gun was cleaned then, because that was the only time 'Old Gertie', as it was nicknamed by Frank, was cleaned the whole time he was in Borneo.

Two days later Wigzell had another run-in with Harrisson. He had made contact with an aircraft with his high-frequency walkie-talkie, and learned that the pilot was looking for Semut 2. Wigzell identified his group, which indicated to the pilot that he was off course.

Harrisson arrived at the wireless sulap and said: 'Did you see the aircraft flying overhead?'

Major Tom Harrisson with a Kelabit native.

'I've just been talking to the pilot,' said Wigzell.

'How did you make contact?' said Harrisson.

With some satisfaction, Wigzell told Harrisson that his radio set had the same frequency as the aircraft.

'If I had known that at the start of the operation,' yelled Harrisson, 'we could have been saved a considerable amount of time and embarrassment.' And he walked away in disgust.

Harrisson now was wearing a type of T-shirt, a wrap-around sarong and belt, native beads around his neck, a wrist watch, and he carried a 1.8 m staff walking stick. During the whole time he was in the interior, Wigzell rarely saw Harrisson carry any weapons. He was usually surrounded by many fierce-looking natives, who were usually armed with evil-looking jungle parangs and blow-pipes with poisoned darts.

The following day as the ground-to-air signal beacon 'Eureka Rebecca' was not in use, Wigzell made contact with a DC3 Dakota aircraft. It was in the wrong valley so he radioed it to gain height and proceed due north. He was rewarded for his efforts with a waggle of the wings when it passed over the wireless sulap.

On his fourth day in Borneo he was summoned to headquarters by a runner from Harrisson. Harrisson questioned him on his service in the Pacific, and seemed quite surprised to learn that he had spent such a lengthy time on operation service with the New Zealanders. To Wigzell's surprise, Harrisson made him a roving wireless operator and operative. Wigzell was to set up a new network of outstations with a base station in the Sarawak area. This new base was to be in operation in a few days' time after the arrival of Captain Gordon Richter, of the Australian Infantry Forces. Wigzell's orders were as follows:

1. Select 10 guerillas from the Belawit area. Arm them with .303 rifles, US Carbines and Owen sub-machine-guns.
2. Obtain an ATR4 radio set from the wireless sulap on the strip.
3. Move via Ba Kelalan, Pa Pala and Long Beluyu into the Padas area of British North Borneo. Continue northward to Long Miau and contact Major Ian Lloyd of the Allied Translation and Interpretation Service (ATIS) who is deciphering Japanese documents there. He will return to Belawit headquarters.
4. You will set up radio communications with Pa Pala, relaying runners' messages from Colin McPherson situated in the Eburu or Bole area. You will not disclose your being in the area there, and not be permitted to join any party of 'Z'.

5. Further instructions will be related to you at a later date.

So ended Wigzell's stay with Australian Bob Long in the Bawang Valley, which was just over the border in Belawit in Dutch Borneo. He now embarked on his long trek northwards. Wigzell had been given a 60 cm square silk map of the area. It was easy to pack and was not easily destroyed, but it was of little use.

On the morning of the second day Wigzell awoke early, sweating and feverish. They were at Pa Pala, and there was still a long way to go.

'Oh no,' he thought to himself, 'it must be malaria.' He was annoyed with himself as the attack could have been prevented by taking his atebrine

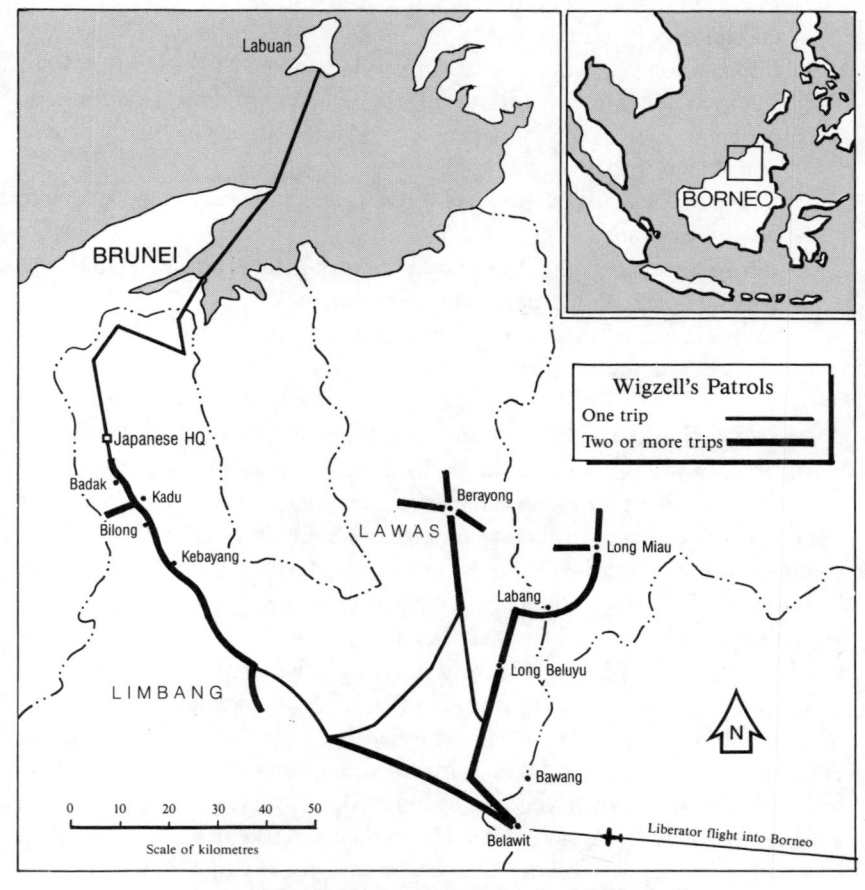

Map showing the trips made by Frank Wigzell.

tablets. For the next 24 hours he lay sweating and delirious. The natives who were with him cared for him and gave him boiled bark water. This was similar to quinine, and was an old native remedy. At the end of this time, it started to take effect. The next day he felt much better and although weak, was able to continue on his travels to Long Miau.

It was at Pa Pala that the first native court was held under tribal customs. Those on trial were the collaborators and informers to the Japanese. Several had been shot and executed by parang under tribal laws. Sentences were imposed under the following classifications:

1. Information given to the enemy but no Japanese punishment inflicted on tribespeople.
   Ruling: Informer severely reprimanded for such practice, and loss of certain tribal rights.
2. Information regarding secrets in the area given to the enemy, food stocks availability, locations in the jungle, guiding Japanese for personal gain and monetary gains and benefits. No Japanese punishment incurred.
   Ruling: All tribal benefits taken away, and warned if reoccurrence, death by parang.
3. Information given to the enemy resulting in reprisals against the tribespeople, causing death and punishment.
   Ruling: Death by shooting by fellow members of the tribe, and in many cases beheading with the parang.

After Wigzell had tracked through Ba Kelalan and Pa Pala he finally contacted Major Ian Lloyd of the ATIS. Lloyd was an Intelligence Officer of the Australian 9th Division on loan to 'Z' to decipher documents held at Long Miau. Lloyd was thrilled to meet another Englishman with whom he could converse in English, as he did not speak Malay. Up until this time he had managed by sign language. Wigzell and his party stayed at the temporary longhouse on the eastern side of the river, and that night he spoke to the natives in Malay. He told them of the impending arrival of approximately 2000 Japanese from Brunei, who were under the command of General Haragushi. These Japanese had been attacked in the Limbang operation on the 7 June at Ukong, by Australian Fred Sanderson, and they had retired to the down-river area of Bukit Malu, crossed the river in force, and had cut a new track 24 km inland from the coast towards Lawas and then headed for the Sapong Rubber Estate to escape the invasion in that area by the Australian 9th Division. It was here that a last stand was to be implemented at the headquarters of the 32nd Japanese Army controlled by General Masao Baba.

Wigzell advised the Kampong Kepala (head man) to vacate the longhouse immediately before the arrival of the Japanese. The Kepala said that he knew of a secure location in the dense jungle not too far away, so Wigzell set up the radio and contact was made immediately with the new Ba Kelalan sub-base.

Major Lloyd now returned to headquarters, having failed to contact Colin McPherson. McPherson was the 'Z' Australian operative in the Eburu Padas area in British North Borneo. The old Kepala of Long Miau area was disinclined to send a search party into this area, as it was a Tagal tribal domain. The Tagals were an untrustworthy tribe and had previously surrendered two United States Air Force men to the Japanese. Their reward was the heads of the airmen.

About this time Wigzell had his first introduction to headhunting during his travels through the many kampongs. Each kampong displayed the bleached skulls from the rafters of the longhouses for all to see. When he returned to the kampongs again at a later date, he would notice several new wicker and reed baskets hanging above the smoky fireplaces. The heads would be smoked above the fireplace and, when Wigzell enquired, much to the delight of the natives he was told that these new heads had been acquired by the younger generation who were following the old rituals and customs of their forefathers.

Many Japanese had lost their lives in Borneo through over-consumption of the local rice wine, borak. Once intoxicated, the Japanese were easy game for the natives, who liquidated them as reprisals for the many atrocities committed against them. The natives had been treated with utter contempt by the Japanese, who had slaughtered the natives in great numbers. Even the lowest-ranked Japanese soldier would kill at the slightest provocation, and not be reprimanded by his officers. It was no wonder then, with the supply of arms and ammunition from the men of 'Z', that the natives took revenge for the shabby treatment they had endured from the Japanese over the previous three years.

Wigzell was glad he was on the natives' side, as the well-built, muscular, native warriors appeared to be very menacing. Their ear-lobes were pierced with large hornbill carvings and leopard teeth, and heavy ornaments hung to their shoulders. They wore ancient glass-bead necklaces, and under each knee was tied a certain species of creeper, which was twisted and secured and of many colours. Copper or aluminium bangles hung from their wrists. The women wore only a black sarong, and were bare above the waist. They wore much the same ornaments as the men. Their hair was cut to the shoulder, and they often wore a conical skull bead-hat on their heads. The men wore only loin cloths, made from three lengths of material.

At first Wigzell gave away the panels from the parachute, but soon he found they were handy as trade objects with the natives as they were in great demand. The natives would make up the green and white material and use it for sarongs to be worn on special occasions.

Wigzell was now in the Padas area of Central Borneo. The Padas was leech infested and disease ridden, and the slightest cut became septic immediately. Even today, people do not travel into the interior of Sarawak, and particularly the Padas area of Sabah. Wigzell's supply of drugs in his first-aid kit was limited to aspro, sulphaguanaine, sulphaanilimide, sulphamerazine, atebrine, iodine, bandages and a few benzedrine tablets. Many of the local tribes were badly infested with sores and leech bites which had turned septic, so each morning Wigzell would hold a sick parade. All the natives would attend, sick or not. Some wanted only to be noticed — Wigzell would give them aspirins! Malaria was rife throughout the area and there were insufficient supplies of atebrine.

By now Frank had grown a beard, partly as a protection against mosquitoes which were rife in the interior, and his skin was turning yellow through taking the atebrine.

Native runners were now appearing with messages from the northern and western areas with the news that the Japanese were advancing from the Brunei Bay location. The locals knew that Wigzell's wireless transmitter was at Long Miau, so all runners were diverted there. A sulap, which had initially been built in the jungle about 140 m from the longhouse, and was completely hidden from view, became the sleeping quarters and the wireless transmitting position for Wigzell's party. About a week after transmissions, Frank heard a Betty reconnaissance plane overhead. Every time he went on the air it seemed to home in on his signals in a direct line for the kampong. He finally came to the conclusin that the aircraft was working in direct contact with the approaching Japanese force below, who were trying to locate the exact position of the radio station. This continued for another day, and then at 5 a.m. the following morning, when they had just woken up in the sulap, they heard the sound of approaching aircraft flying in from the north-west. The aircraft seemed to be coming in very low, and it looked as though they were headed straight for them.

'Japon kapal terbang!' [Jap aircraft], shouted Wigzell. 'Those bastards are coming straight for us! Disana!' [There, i.e. get down.]

They all hit the floor, and just in the nick of time as two fighter-bombers made a 180-degree turn behind them, and headed straight for the longhouse, each dropping two bombs. Fortunately, the pilot's aim was inaccurate, the bombs missed them completely, and there was no damage or injury in the kampong. The aircraft did not return but continued flying directly northwest. Wigzell concluded that the aircraft must have been short of fuel.

Just as the men were recovering an Iban arrived who told them that he had sighted the Japanese. He had circled around them in the jungle and come straight to Wigzell. Frank reckoned that the Japanese were approximately 1½ hours away. They had little time left. He immediately coded a message on the wireless and reported to headquarters, and was ordered to clear the area. They did this just in time. The party crossed the river by perahu, and just missed the advance party of the Japanese. While still in the cover of the jungle they could see the Japanese advancing in single file upon the now-unoccupied longhouse on the hill.

Wigzell and his party moved stealthily to the south trail and had gone some 300 m when they heard a terrific crashing through the undergrowth from above, and coming from the kampong area. They nearly jumped out of their skins as a water buffalo came thundering down the hill through the secondary growth and headed for the safety of the jungle below them. If they had had the misfortune to have been in its path, nothing would have saved them from certain death.

The men guessed that the beast had been disturbed by the Japanese, so they jumped off the track and followed the path of the downward trail of the buffalo. This was to cover their tracks, and then they headed for the river. It was obvious by now that they had been sighted by the Japanese who were approaching the longhouse. The leading Kelabit, who knew this area well, found an old disused trail near the river, and they all followed silently and cautiously for the next hour, heading due south.

They approached the main track again, searched the ground for Japanese movement, then immediately set up their standard patrol procedure of one scout in advance and rear protection. Wigzell and his men now rapidly retreated across rivers and valleys, and finally arrived in the central Sarawak safety area, Ba Kelalan, in 15 hours instead of the usual two days. The natives were amazed that Wigzell was fit enough to keep up with them, but he had been helped on the long trek by some benzedrine tablets from the medical kit.

When the exhausted men arrived at the temporary headquarters, they were greeted with a warm welcome and a cup of coffee. This was the first drink they had had, other than water, since leaving Belawit. It was sheer luxury to be able to lie down and catch up on much-needed sleep.

Eventually Tom Harrisson arrived, and presented Wigzell with a badge in the form of a shield to wear on his shirt lapel. This was in blue and gold with the Sarawak coat of arms. 'This gives you the equivalent rank of Major in the Sarawak Armed Forces,' he told Wigzell.

However, Wigzell was inclined not to believe him, and he knew that the natives would not be impressed with the badge or understand it.

When Wigzell had fully recovered from the trip, and with two additional carriers for the wireless gear, he and his guerillas were ordered to the Lawas area to report to Lieutenant Bob Pinkerton of the Australian Infantry Forces. Pinkerton had requested Wigzell's help, as his group in the coastal region of Lawas was experiencing communication problems. Wigzell had previously met Pinkerton at Fraser Island and knew he was a much-respected man.

Pa Berayong was a four-day walk to the west. On the third day they arrived at a small kampong of 15 families to be greeted with the news that rice and food were scarce and there was an absence of game.

The Murut villagers at this kampong were good gardeners, but their maize crop was not ready to be harvested. News came before dusk that a small herd of sika or samba deer had been sighted upstream.

'Come on, Prank,' said the natives in Malay. (They could not pronounce the letter 'F'.) 'Help us get a deer for food.'

Light was fading by the time Frank and two natives approached the garden in search of the deer. With a trusty .303 rifle belonging to one of the home-guards of the area, Wigzell was able to get within 30 m of the deer. He took aim and fired, and that night they all sat down to a delectable meal.

The venison had been cooked in a Chinese wok, and was a little tougher than normal, but what a change from rice! Frank had been continually eating rice and he missed salt, which was priceless and scarce in this part of Borneo. The Japanese had requested that all fruit, rice and meat be sent to their forces on the coastal areas, and the natives were paid in Japanese occupational currency for this.

After the meal of deer and borak the men slept soundly in the kampong. At night the kampong dogs ran riot within the longhouses, and Wigzell always took the precaution of hanging all his clothes out of their reach, as they chewed anything containing salt. Some of the other operatives had lost clothes to the dogs this way.

At several places in the interior salt springs were known to exist. Large trays filled with salt-springs water were exposed to sunlight, and by a process of evaporation small amounts were extracted from the briny waters with each session.

After the arrival of the 'Z' operatives and the consolidation of the interior, all transportation of food — rice, meat, fish, vegetables, fowls, and fruit — was discontinued. The Japanese issued notices stating that, if the transportation of food was not recommenced, the natives would be dealt with severely for disobeying orders. Much to the pleasure of all the tribes, the Japanese patrols were allowed to journey several days away into the interior from their headquarters. They were then killed by the natives, who now possessed modern weapons and had been taught how to use them.

Japanese heads were now plentiful and hung from the rafters of the longhouses in small reed and rattan boxes above the smoky fireplaces. These heads were the prized possessions of the natives.

The local pigs who lived under the longhouses fed on excretia that came from above during the night, and quite often the 'Z' operatives would comment when they ate the pork that it tasted like the matter the pigs fed on. It was a rarity for the men to eat any sort of meat, but sometimes they would have an occasional monkey or snake. Crocodile steaks were a rarity.

About this time Wigzell was approached by a young 16-year-old Kelabit named John. Since Wigzell had arrived in the kampong, John had followed him around, and now he shyly plucked up courage and asked to join Wigzell's party. He expressed his loyalty and a willingness to show bravery in attacking the Japanese. He was soon to prove that this was no understatement. Wigzell liked this young boy and knew instinctively he would be an asset. He gave John his only spare weapon, an Owen sub-machine-gun, some web gear and some ammunition.

Next morning the journey northwards towards Lawas continued. In the afternoon, while climbing towards Pa Berayong, Wigzell met up with Australians Bill Nibbs and Joe da Roza, who had arrived in Borneo with him. The Japanese had just taken over Pa Berayong, and Bill and his guerillas had just completed a reconnaissance of that area.

Wigzell set up the wireless and contacted central base requesting a supply drop and RAAF attack on that area. He and his party decided to join forces with Nibbs and da Roza, and they took a jungle track over the mountain and advanced on Pa Berayong. On the way they had two potentially fatal encounters. On a steep track the advanced scout indicated that there was trouble ahead, and John told Wigzell that red bull ants, which Wigzell had never encountered before, were falling from the 30 m trees along the track. They could inflict severe pain as the sting was like being touched by a red-hot poker. Unfortunately, Wigzell and three of the natives were stung badly, but immediately the natives cut a water vine and applied the liquid to the bite which deadened the pain.

Continuing northwards, they came to an area where the track took a new turn to the left off the main one, and was marked with a forked stick, indicating that the old track was not to be used. John explained that a monster lurked in the defined area, and superstition prevented anyone entering such places where marked. Wigzell told the natives that he intended to investigate this area, but they anxiously replied, 'Tidah Tuan' [No, sir].

Wigzell went forward with the fearless John and two others following more cautiously. Suddenly the three natives pointed to an overhanging branch above the track. Their eyes were wide and staring, and they were speechless. There, hanging motionless, and perfectly camouflaged in the jungle environment, was a huge green python with black stripes. Wigzell froze in his tracks and, as if in a dream, he fired two shots from his US carbine. The python fell on to the track, and the natives dashed forward and beheaded it. The forked sticks were now disposed of at the junction of the trails, and the men proceeded on their way, much to the delight of the guerillas, who still thought that the local superstitions should have been observed in that particular case.

Wigzell and John with three other Kelabits now approached Pa Berayong. Suddenly John beckoned urgently to Wigzell to approach him quietly, and indicated that five Japanese were in front of him on the trail. Cautiously Wigzell approached John, and looking around a bend of the track he could see the Japanese with their backs to them. With their hearts beating fast, Wigzell and John took two steps out into the centre of the path, and immediately the Japanese turned and faced them. Simultaneously, Wigzell and John opened fire, and three Japanese fell to the ground mortally wounded. The other two escaped over the embankment on to the track leading towards the river and Tengoa Valley. Three of Wigzell's party immediately gave chase, but lost their quarry, who now hid in the thick undergrowth nearby. The operatives' cover was blown, and their only hope was to return to the other side of the range and set up an ambush in the event of being followed. However, nothing further happened, and they retired into the jungle for concealment.

Later that afternoon, shattering the peace of the jungle, a squadron of RAAF Kittyhawks flew over. The operatives identified themselves with a hand-signalling mirror. A note was dropped from the planes asking where the enemy were and, by unravelling a toilet roll in a deserted kampong clearing, Frank traced out the Japanese positions and the direction in which the Japanese were travelling. This was acknowleges by a waggle of wings, and the aircraft flew off in that direction.

At that moment, to Wigzell's surprise and delight, a group of his old New Zealand friends whom he had left at Morotai — Frank Leckie, Jack Butt and George Edlin — arrived. After a great welcome, they all proceeded back over the range and found that the Japanese had left the area. They contacted central base, giving details of the action with the Japanese, and then divided into three parties in search of the retreating Japanese. Leckie took the bottom trail, and Wigzell the top; about 500 metres of jungle separated them both. They failed to see any Japanese but they did notice boot tracks on the soft earth.

Suddenly the quietness of the jungle was shattered by a burst of machine-gun fire from a Bren gun. Frank Leckie's group had approached two rear Japanese guards, and Leckie and two Kelabits, armed with pistols and parangs, intended to take them silently. Unfortunately, the Japanese had seen Leckie and reached for their weapons. At the crucial moment Jack Butt had come to his assistance and killed both Japanese with one short burst with the Bren.

In the meantime Wigzell's group had not been idle. They came across a small sulap in a clearing. This time John led the party, but he was soon back at Wigzell's side, and said: 'Tuan — Japoon tinggal dalam sulap disana.' ('Careful Frank — there are Japs in the sulap over there.')

The door of the sulap was closed and the shutters drawn, but the men could see a Japanese rifle leaning against the hut. Also, the natives, with their keen hearing, could hear Japanese voices coming from within. Cautiously, they approached, and the boys covered the doorway in a semicircle from the jungle, and three went up the trail ahead in case there should be further Japanese arriving from that area if firing should break out.

Wigzell swapped his carbine for an Owen and two magazines, and made for the doorway with John. He indicated to John that he would kick the door open, as it was ajar a few inches, and not to use a grenade, but both spray right and left with their Owens. There was no time to think. His actions relied purely on reflex and his Fraser Island training. As the two men fired inside the sulap, bodies slumped to the earth floor, and they continued to fire until the 28 rounds in the magazines had run out.

Slightly sickened by the sight of all the blood, Wigzell went out into the fresh jungle air and gave the order to his men: 'Ambil orang Japoon disini dari sulap.' ('Bring the Japs from the hut.')

He certainly wasn't prepared for the next event that took place. There was suddenly a mad rush to comply with this order. With shouts of 'Baik, baik, baik,' and with their arms raised in the air as though holding weapons of ancient times, Wigzell was greeted with the sight of four Muruts holding above their heads trophies of the hunt — the heads of the recently killed Japanese.

Frank's face turned green and he wanted to be sick. 'Ye gods!' he thought. 'What have I got myself into?'

But all he could do with these smiling and laughing guerillas was to comply with the age-old ritual, and hold his gun aloft and join the chant.

CHAPTER 11

Living with the Headhunters of Borneo

*'Take the crest of a mountain and stone by stone mount
And every stone you tread, one more struggle count.'*

CRETAN MANTINADE

After this action with the Japanese, Wigzell and his men returned to Pa Berayong, as their whereabouts were now known to the Japanese in the area. A circle of Muruts, Kelabits, and Ibans were placed around the kampong at Pa Berayong for security. Wigzell was given control of a small army mortar and with the rest of his group was to protect the escape route over the mountain. He used the radio to advise central headquarters of their situation, and was told that a RAAF aircraft had gone down in the jungle somewhere to the east of their kampong. Wigzell said that he would keep a lookout for the aircraft.

A third patrol led by Bill Nibbs from the Australian Infantry Forces took the trail to Lawas via Pa Tengoa to see if the area was clear of Japanese. On the second day out, accompanied by a Murut called Sabal, Nibbs negotiated a 30–40 metre stretch of straight-line track. Until then they had had no contact with the enemy. Without any warning, they came under sudden fire from a Japanese light machine-gun. It was just as well for Nibbs and his group of guerillas that the machine-gun had been incorrectly set up and elevated too high, because the first burst of fire missed the party completely. Nibbs and Sabal were uninjured, and dived off the track into a small ravine. They then retreated further into the jungle, while the rest of the guerillas engaged the enemy before returning to Pa Berayong.

When two days had gone by, and Wigzell had still not heard from Nibbs and Sabal, he advised Harrisson by radio that he thought the two men must be considered lost in action, the first of Semut 1. In the meantime, Wigzell sent out patrols to locate the Japanese, but there were no signs of any.

After four days in the jungle, Nibbs was starting to think they were never going to find their way back to Pa Berayong, but just when he had almost given up hope Sabal recognised an area that he knew well. They all returned to Pa Berayong shortly after to a great welcome.

During Nibbs' absence, Wigzell had received a message over the radio from central base for Nibbs. The decoded text was 'kill or be killed' and this worried Wigzell. It was not in conformity with the practices and known principles of 'Z' Special Unit. Wigzell decided to question Harrisson on this, but he denied sending the message. In later years, Wigzell was to find out from other members of 'Z' that they had received the same message.

In the next few days, the two Japanese that had eluded Wigzell's party on the track over the mountains were captured and brought to the kampong. In halting Malay the Japanese requested to be delivered to their own medical officer as they were undernourished and rife with malaria and beri-beri. They had travelled a long distance since leaving Brunei in the south, moving as inconspicuously as possible to avoid detection. Wigzell and the other 'Z' operatives had been instructed by Tom Harrisson to take no prisoners within Borneo in the initial stages of their operation, because if the prisoners escaped the operatives would probably have been discovered, and the natives executed for assisting them. There was nothing else that Wigzell could do — the natives took the two unfortunate Japanese for a long walk in the jungle.

Each operative in his own area had direct control and exercised his own judgment in any emergency. This method of operating was essential, as delay in most cases would have meant severe casualties. Rank was of no importance to the operatives within Borneo; they were all classified as loners who made their own plans and carried them out.

There was no contact with any other Europeans, and in most cases they had to depend on the tribes to co-operate and share everything they had. Each operative carried with him a potassium cyanide capsule, to be taken in the event of capture and torture by the Japanese. This was also to ensure that they would not give away valuable information to the enemy such as names of people, places, dates etc. During training all SOA personnel were instructed not to fraternise with the other SOA members as, in the event of their capture, they could not give away any information about the other operatives. They knew they were all expendable.

All the 'Z' operatives were advised before going on any operations that contact by them with their next-of-kin would be impossible from occupied territories, and that once a month SRD and 'Z' Special Unit's headquarters would telegram their families to advise that they were fit and well. Unfortunately, this never happened, and most of the operatives' relatives were never contacted by 'Z' Special Unit or SRD.

On the afternoon following the day the two sick Japanese prisoners disappeared for ever, the men heard rifle fire from the river bank, and as previously agreed upon, they all went to their various patrol stations. Wigzell positioned the mortar to cover the lower area from where the enemy would appear and set up the Bren gun and mortar with young John and his group. Nothing further eventuated until the men noticed Frank Leckie arriving back from the river location, followed by many tribesmen carrying a body.

According to Leckie, his natives had seen an unidentified person in uniform approaching the kampong who fired upon them. The natives immediately returned the fire, and the man was killed. Sadly, the victim was identified as the pilot of the RAAF aircraft that had previously crashed in the jungle. Having survived the crash, he had apparently headed down the river towards the coast where he had run into the natives. His aircraft was never found and Wigzell was allotted the task of making a headboard for his grave. He traced the details on a piece of local timber, and his natives copied the pencil markings with a hot iron rod. The identification was then burned on to the headboard to provide a record until the War Graves Commission could recover the body. The Australian was buried in the kampong grounds.

Tom Harrisson was advised by radio of the pilot's death and arrived promptly a couple of days later, having been in the forward area of Sarawak when the radio signal was received at central headquarters. He duly advised the Royal Australian Air Force.

As had happened previously when Harrisson arrived, Wigzell was given his marching orders for another long walk. He was not to continue to Lawas, but to head south-west to the junction of the Limbang and Pa Brunot track. By now, Wigzell was wondering if Harrisson really enjoyed giving these orders and causing so much disharmony amongst the operatives. His orders were to meet up with Australian Fred Sanderson en route to the Limbang River and to obtain another radio as he had left his behind with George Edlin at Pa Berayong.

Wigzell met Fred Sanderson at the junction of the Pa Berayong and Limbang tracks — a journey of two days. Sanderson, who had fought in the Middle East, and been a member of the Rats of Tobruk, was 35 years of age, 1.71 m tall, lean and olive-skinned. He had arrived in Borneo before Wigzell, having been one of the first members of Semut 1, and was strong, immensely capable and outspoken. On meeting Sanderson's party now, however, Wigzell discovered that they were not carrying a radio set, so he was forced to spend another 2½ days walking to Belawit HQ to collect one, together with spares.

During this time Wigzell again met up with Bob Long and the American Dan Urlich, who was just about ready to fly home by Auster aircraft, after being reported missing in action over Borneo. On board the incoming Auster was a brand-new Boston Mk 3 radio with field generator and the necessary spare parts.

'It won't need to be tested, Frank,' said Bob Long. 'It's just been checked at Labuan.'

Wigzell accepted Long's word and walked over to the supply depot to re-equip his guerillas with ammunition.

'Hey, where do you think you're going?' asked Harrisson when he saw where Wigzell was heading.

'I'm getting more clothes and money, and more ammunition for my men,' said Wigzell.

'Well, you're not allowed in there,' said an irate Harrisson. 'You'll have to make do with what you've got.'

Wigzell swore under his breath. What a bastard the man was! He was probably going to open a bank with the gold coins and trading monies, he thought.

As time went on, Wigzell and the other 'Z' operatives found out more

Muruts of North Borneo.

about Tom Harrisson. He had a palatial private sulap containing beds, chairs, tables, and every imaginable comfort. Six attractive young Kelabit girls, aged between 12-14 attended to his every need. He was known as Tuan Rajah Tom, for the natives believed that only a King or Rajah would wear a crown on his shoulders (when he was in uniform, the natives noticed Harrisson's Major's crown on his shoulders.) He had made a point of telling all the operatives of Semut 1 that there was to be no fraternisation with the women of Borneo but he was the first to break this order.

Wigzell's party was now increased to 18, with a new addition to the fighting guerillas — Ranu, a young friend of John's. Ranu was full of energy, and was a welcome addition to the group.

The advance to the Limbang was a long and hazardous journey, made all the more dangerous as the operatives had just heard that the Japanese were moving towards the Limbang in substantial numbers from the Semut 2 area — Toby Carter's group. The trails to the Limbang were saturated and soggy after heavy rainfall. These were treacherous conditions for fast movement. There were six small streams to ford, and one large one was so flooded that it took a long time to cross. The men used a 2 metre wooden staff to assist them against the flow of the water. They only just made it to the other side.

Just off the track before reaching Pa Brunot, Fred Sanderson told Wigzell about a hidden store in the jungle filled with tins of 03 rations and .303 rifles. Wigzell pounced on them as if they were buried treasure and had no compunction in removing them all, as ammunition was in very short supply. It was just as well he did so because, even though he did not know it then, he and his men were never to receive a supply drop of arms or ammunition in Limbang.

At the junction of the Pa Berayong-Limbang trail, the men stayed at a sulap, and while the others rested for a while Wigzell decided to test the new Boston radio. He assembled it and then tried to operate it. Nothing happened.

'Damn and blast,' swore Wigzell. 'It's my own fault for not testing it earlier.'

The radio would transmit but not receive. Never again would he trust anything without trying it first. He suddenly had an idea of interchanging the slide-out mechanism tray with that of George Edlin's useless Boston radio left in the sulap. When he did this, he switched to receive and was elated to find it now worked perfectly.

The men finally arrived at the kampong of Pa Brunot wet and exhausted. But it turned out to be an excellent kampong in which to recover after such a long ordeal. It was a Sunday, and all the Christian Muruts were going to

A Murut girl playing a bamboo flute.

a small church sulap near the river. After changing out of his dirty clothes, Wigzell joined them, and was given an important seat in the congregation. It was a seat usually reserved for visitors on the platform beside the minister, who was a native Kiai, or learned one. Wigzell was asked to read an excerpt from the Bible in Malay, and when he had finished, he was given a rousing reception. This was the first time a white man had taken an active part in a church service before in this area of Sarawak.

All the woman of the tribe had dressed in pure white dresses for this special occasion. These dresses had been made before the Japanese invasion, and probably in the time of the missionaries. The men wore shorts and shirts, and once the Church service was over the women immediately reverted to their usual sarong, for the temperature in this valley was 104 degrees in the shade.

The kampong was very clean and tidy, with about 20 families who were well-educated and excellent gardeners. Wigzell never ceased to be amazed at the prolific growth and glorious colours of the wild flowers in the dense jungle, especially the orchids growing on the tree trunks. He was given a conducted tour of the valley, and together with his two young guerillas, John and Manu, was treated with great friendliness. When he was offered a swim he jumped at the chance, and much to the delight of the natives, stripped off and dived into the cool river.

He was amazed to find that after the swim his skin, which had turned dark brown by travelling through the jungle without a shirt, had turned white. His tan had vanished. The natives just stared at his white body, amazed at the colour of his skin. His beard was very long, so one of the tribesmen produced a sharp hunting knife and trimmed it. Wigzell was a little apprehensive at this, for if the knife should slip he would surely have been hung from the rafters in one of the reed baskets above the smoky fireplaces!

The next part of the trek to the Limbang River was the hardest and most demanding that Wigzell was ever to encounter in Borneo. The party started to climb a high mountain range of about 900 metres. This took all day from early dawn at 4.30 a.m. to mid-evening at 8.30 p.m. When they finally reached the summit, the men were exhausted, but they were met by the most amazing sight. A huge crack in the earth's surface stretched for kilometres along the mountain ridge, which gave the impression that it had been created by an earthquake of great magnitude thousands of years before. The natives had formed a clearing in this spot, but there was a gap of perhaps 7 or 8 metres. This was bridged by two large trees, each about 13 metres in length. Wigzell's men ran across this, but one boy who was carrying the radio nearly overbalanced with the extra weight of the Boston.

Wigzell was told to wait until the others had crossed before crossing the gap. With sweat pouring down his face, and with his heart in his mouth, he somehow managed to get across, with cheers of encouragement by the natives. They camped in that area for the night, and then proceeded down the mountain track early the next morning. On arrival at Kepala Tamabo Sarawka's kampong (the name means 'Great Mountain of Sarawak') at Ulu Limbang, Wigzell found that Fred Sanderson's party had left that very morning by perahu for the Iban longhouse of Bilong, one day's travel down the river.

No Japanese had been reported in the immediate vicinity of this Murut location. Wigzell's party had made good progress, catching up on the lost seven days. Wigzell assembled the Boston and slung the aerial between two large trees near the longhouse. As they were situated between two large mountain ridges, he decided to see if his old New Zealand theory of bounce and skip transmission would work. Eureka! Not only did it work (much to the surprise of base headquarters as well), but contact was made on the first 'sked'. The signals were crystal clear and of maximum strength.

Wigzell's message to base was sharp and to the point. They were at the Ulu Limbang, but could not continue downstream until Sanderson's boats returned. Tom Harrisson was at the radio hut at Belawit, and gave the radio operator curt instructions to inform Wigzell to proceed by foot. Not to be outdone, Wigzell immediately informed base that the only method of travel in that remote part of Borneo was by perahu, and he did not intend to leave for another two days. Wigzell received no reply to this, so he presumed that Harrisson was satisfied.

It was at the kampong at Ulu Limbang that Wigzell encountered his first real dose of amoebic dysentery. Up until then he had been lucky, but dysentery was rife in that part of the country. The local Kepala and three members of his family had recently died from the disease, probably caused by urine seeping into the well beside the longhouse. Wigzell thought he was going to die too. For three days he lay sweating, feverish and with a high temperature, hardly able to drink the water given to him by sympathetic natives. They bathed his forehead and administered heavy doses of sulphaguanadine from his medical kit, which gradually brought the dysentery under control. At its worst stage he passed large quantities of blood, which weakened his physical condition, which up until then had been strong and healthy. The guerillas had built a seat and dug a hole beside a tree close to the sleeping hut, and during the night a rope to the tree supported him. The men covered him with a blanket to protect him from the mosquitoes, which to Frank seemed as big as DC3 Dakotas. A loyal native stood on guard close beside him just in case any roving Japanese infiltrated the area. Even today Wigzell describes the pain from his rectum as similar to being burnt by a blow torch!

When the worst of the dysentery had subsided Wigzell, although still weak and ill, managed to take a walk with John and Ranu. They visited a small village in which was one of the worst kampongs he was ever to see in Borneo. It consisted of about 10 families, mostly lazy Muruts, who were heavy borak drinkers for most of the year until the wine ran out. These Muruts were undernourished, and lived in dirty conditions with little sense of responsibility, and no personal hygiene. No one ventured outside at night, and those who needed to relieve themselves would squat over an open trapdoor in the longhouse. Mainstream and river areas had a bamboo walkway 30 metres out into the river, and about two-and-a-half metres above the water line, with a couple of bamboo rods forming a seat. This was not used when the Japanese were about as a person sitting on the seat would have been an excellent target.

Shortly after this John and Ranu tracked a hornbill and killed it with Wigzell's Carbine. The hornbill weighed nearly three kilograms and after it was dressed and boiled it made a delicious soup. Frank found the soup nourishing and began to feel a little better. He even managed to eat most of the flesh too.

About this time Frank sewed his cyanide capsule into the left lapel of his jungle shirt. It was better to be safe than sorry, he thought. After all, he had had a close experience with the Japanese at Long Miau, and now he was in completely unknown area, which had only just recently been penetrated by Sanderson, his new partner. Sanderson was the first white man ever seen there.

The Japanese were not his only worry at this time. The lethal piranha fish with their razor-sharp teeth, peculiar to the tropics, together with crocodiles, infested the rivers. Large pythons were common, and all these were peculiar to the Ulu Limbang area. Luckily, the men had left behind the diseased area of Central Sarawak which was infested with leeches. The leeches would stick to the body like glue and would have to be burned off.

Sanderson's perahu party finally returned to Ulu Limbang, and Frank's party now commenced the journey down its swollen rivers. There had been torrential rain over the last few days, and it was difficult to control the perahus. The flow of the water was about 6-7 knots, which made paddling almost impossible. The men just managed to steer the perahu, and Wigzell, sitting in the bow of the leading boat, kept a keen eye out for any pigs, which made easy targets as the perahus were silent. When he saw one asleep on a ledge he shot it. As the boats moved along the river, the natives fished, and caught many types of fish that Wigzell had never seen before,

By this time it was 11 July 1945. Wigzell arrived at Rumah Kadu on 15 July. Rumah Kadu was 25 minutes downriver from Bilong, and was inhabited by native Ibans. These Ibans were part of the Tabon tribe, and were great supporters of the original party of 'Z' operatives who came to Borneo. They were well built, with light-olive skins and were supreme fighters.

Fred Sanderson, who had arrived at Rumah Bilong before Wigzell, stayed with 5 families of this tribe on the north side of the river, while Wigzell stayed with 30 families at Penghulu Kadu's longhouse. After settling in at the longhouse, Wigzell made contact with headquarters in the interior of Sarawak, and soon realised that wireless operations in this area were a hit-or-miss affair, as had so often happened in other areas. The quality and transmission in the Rumah Kadu Limbang River area was exceptional. It had always been presumed that contact could not be effected from the Limbang but Wigzell had now proved that theory wrong. However, there were some Australians from the 9th Division down the river at Ukong who had never successfully operated a radio set in Borneo, and therefore could not transmit or receive messages in their location.

In using his Boston receiver, Wigzell managed to locate two stations which transmitted music — one from Tarakan, and the other in the Philippines. The natives were amazed at this, and sat listening to the music, their eyes wide with wonder. They had never heard music from a wireless set in their lives, and from then on Wigzell was known as Tuan Pukal Wireless Prank. Help was now always available to operate his radio pedal generator.

With a break from action, it was wonderful to relax at this kampong. There were no Japanese in the area and, as it was about a week since he had left Pa Brunot, Wigzell decided that he must have another swim to become human again.

He noticed the Ibans moving down to the river, and he followed them and undressed at the river bank, leaving his weapons there. The Ibans had a strict moral code, and each person when naked would cover the lower part of the body with their hands before entering the water. Only when the water was up to the waist did they remove their hands. At Belawit, Wigzell had managed to find a cake of soap which he now used. The natives could hardly contain their delight, and shouted and laughed. They pointed their arms in his direction and chanted 'Orang Puteh, Orang Puteh' (white man, white man). Several young native girls, aged between 13 and 15, and of marriageable status, chanted: 'Tuan Prank, boleh Kasi sayah kita punya sabun, sayah mahu itu' ('Tuan Frank, please give me your soap, I want it.')

When Wigzell heard this, he replied: 'Mahu itu, fikir kita boleh ambil itu dari sayah?' ('Want it? Do you think you can take it from me?')

He was immediately tackled by many slithering and naked bodies, ducked beneath the water, and held there by two of the laughing girls. With very little trouble, the girls managed to retrieve the soap, and set about giving Wigzell a thorough scrubbing. The screams of delight must have carried far into the jungle that hot afternoon.

There were many such pranks played on the 'Z' men during their time in Borneo. Although magnificent warriors, the Tabon natives were kindly and children at heart. When Wigzell returned from his many patrols and ambushes he would find all his clothes, which by now were threadbare, washed and dried, and neatly arranged on his sleeping mat in the wireless sulap. Three escorting native guerillas, responsible to the Penghulu of the area, were at his side 24 hours a day.

Wigzell was invited to attend a mouse deer hunt at the corn field nearby during the night. The mouse deer is a miniature creature approximately 45 cm tall, and is an exact replica of the larger deer, including the antlers. It lives in the corn fields, is inquisitive, being attracted to light during darkness, and ventures out into open areas surrounding the fields. The natives lit fires, and when the mouse deer were within a range of 30 metres, they shot them with their sumpitans, or blow pipes, using a paralysing poison. The deer's throat was then cut and the blood released to make them edible.

The poisoned darts were completely silent, and other animals were also killed in this way. These darts were used quite often by the natives to kill unsuspecting Japanese. Because of the speed and silence of the darts, the enemy were not able to warn the advancing party.

Small parties of the Japanese were being ambushed and killed in this area continually by the natives. Their bush-telegraphy was constantly at work and because of its efficiency Wigzell and Sanderson knew long before any Japanese approached of their presence in the area. The Japanese had absolutely no chance of survival in small groups. Ambushes were set up well in advance, and the area cleared of any native population. However, the Ibans were inclined to be impatient, and Wigzell and Sanderson constantly had to teach them restraint.

The Ibans, as with all the natives, had a strong sense of smell, and they would know well in advance if Japanese were about. Many times they would use a parang to kill the enemy. The first time Wigzell saw this happen he was amazed at the speed and efficiency with which the natives stalked and killed their quarry. They would creep stealthily up behind an unsuspecting Japanese, fling an arm around his neck, place a hand over his mouth to stop him calling out, and draw the parang from one end of his throat to the other in one quick, silent movement. The Japanese would fall

A group of Iban headhunters.

to the ground without a sound — the whole action taking no more than two or three seconds. The Japanese would never know what had hit him.

There were two kinds of malaria in Borneo. One particularly lethal type was cerebral malaria. The Limbang River was located in a highly infected area known as the 'Seria Malaria District'. While Wigzell was staying there, one young Iban became infected with this disease. The symptoms were similar to the more common type of malaria — high temperature, alternating with cold periods, rapidly increasing over the next two days. The Iban gradually lost consciousness after bouts of uncontrollable raving, then he became delirious and had to be restrained. He finally died about the seventh day. This type of malaria affects the brain, which drowns in its own fluid.

Small parties of Japanese were still appearing in the area, and were quickly disposed of, much to the delight of the Ibans. It seemed to Frank that every native Iban wanted a trophy of the hunt, and he became quite used to seeing the ghastly, bleached skulls hanging on the rafters inside the huts. The first indication that a native warrior was returning from hunting the Japanese was a piercing, ear-shattering tremulous yodel, starting on a low key and gradually increasing to a note that sent a shiver up his spine. This announced to the rest of the tribe that a warrior had returned from the hunt with a trophy — the victim's skull, attached to his belt by its hair or a rattan vine. The warrior then emerged from the jungle holding his weapons aloft, and dressed only in a loin cloth. All the natives stopped working and approached him, paying their respect to an honoured member of their tribe.

Wigzell and Sanderson received the news over the radio that a Japanese force from Belawit had come through the Tutoh into the Semut 1 area. With about 120 Ibans and 17 perahus, Sanderson headed up the Madalam River in pursuit. He was lucky to come out alive. On the journey up the river, one of the Iban scouts spotted a Japanese on the western bank, his rifle raised and aiming straight at the perahu containing Sanderson. The Iban shouted a warning to Sanderson. This may have unnerved the Japanese, for the bullet pierced the perahu only a few centimetres behind Sanderson's seat. For a long time afterward it was a standing joke with Sanderson, who would tell everybody that the Japanese had nearly 'wrecked him' (rectum). 'I nearly got my ass shot off,' he would say. 'Those Nips bloody well nearly killed me!'

Sanderson and the Ibans took to the eastern bank to fight the Japanese, and under cover of fire retrieved 13 of the perahus. The four remaining ones were destroyed and lost.

When Sanderson and his Ibans returned to Rumah Kadu, Wigzell and his men joined them and they all started to patrol the Limbang and Kuala Madalam areas. The Japanese by now had crossed over to the eastern side of the Madalam and began to trek up into the interior near Rumah Kadu. They were getting nearer to the operatives.

The next day, while Wigzell was out on patrol, he saw four Japanese making a raft at the water's edge. He shouted to them, and they immediately disappeared into the jungle and did not return. By now Wigzell and Sanderson were running out of ammunition, and unless their supplies were replenished soon, they would be in a serious position.

Sanderson decided he would try and get some from the Australian 9th Division, the 2/17 Battalion which was now located in the lower Limbang River. This battalion patrol usually came up river by landing boat to the Madalam river mouth and collected the operatives' report once a week. This

A young Dayak girl of Sarawak.

time they gave Sanderson the last of their ammunition; they had no idea when the next supply would come. The Australians from this division were amazed and envious when they saw the operatives with the beautiful bare-breasted young girls from the kampongs, who had travelled down river with the operatives.

> 'Little did they know what it was like living in the interior,' says Wigzell today. 'The last thing on our minds at that stage was hanky-panky with the native girls. We were exceedingly short of ammunition and food, and always worrying about this. It was accepted tribal kampong practice that an honoured visitor should be offered the hospitality of the area, by presenting him with one of their beautiful young maidens during his stay in the area. The native people thought that the introduction of a new blood strain into their community would help regenerate the tribe and diminish the effects of in-breeding within the longhouse. This was offered sincerely to all operatives in Borneo, but it was not taken up. Our major concern was for food and ammunition, not sex.'

The Iban male was reputed to be a talented lover. According to Corporal Roly Griffiths-Marsh, an Australian member of 'Z', some of the young native men had their penises perforated and enlarged by slivers of bamboo above the head. When the wound had healed a silver pin with a ball at each end would be inserted so the pin would not fall out. It was alleged that the Iban woman, when penetrated by a male so equipped, would be provided with exquisite sexual pleasure, and that she could even refuse to marry or seek a divorce from any man who was not equipped with this. Similarly, an eyelid of a wild pig, when slipped over an erect penis, also served the same purpose.

Because of the extreme shortage of ammunition, Wigzell and Sanderson had been instructed that, in the event of being attacked, they were to retire down the river to the Ukong. These instructions were given to them on 1 August 1945. At this date the headquarters at Ukong were under a temporary cease-fire order, and no arms or ammunition were to be supplied to their group. Japan had, as yet, not signed the surrender document to the Allies.

However, surrender pamphlets were now being dropped all over the areas which contained the Japanese force. It was decided to send four Ibans carrying surrender documents to request the Japanese to surrender. There was an immediate reaction. Three of the Ibans were beheaded, and one was sent back slightly wounded with the reply, 'Come out and fight, you white bastards'. The Japanese Commander, Captain Fujin, was convinced the Emperor would never surrender. He thought the news that an atomic bomb had been dropped on his country was an army and political ploy to scare his group, known as Fujino Tai, into surrendering.

CHAPTER 12

The Final Surrender

*'You're sick of the game, well now
that's a shame
You're young and you're brave and
you're bright
You've had a raw deal, I know, but
don't squeal
Buck up your damndest, and fight.'*

SOURCE UNKNOWN

The 'Z' operatives' position in the Limbang was precarious now, as incoming reports from roving Punan natives indicated that the Fujino Tai force was moving up the Limbang into the interior. Wigzell asked in desperation for more ammunition from Tom Harrisson and the Australian 9th Division but the request was denied. Wigzell and Sanderson both decided to remain with their Iban friends and help out in any way possible. Even though there was little ammunition, some of the Ibans' weapons — especially the blowpipe, or sumpitan, as it was known — would be useful in any skirmish with the Japanese.

The two men suspected that the Japanese were soon to mount an attack against their kampong, so they decided to sleep in an outer visitors' sulap near the river, as the river was low and it would be easy for the enemy to cross. In the event of this happening, Wigzell would drop the Boston radio and weighted code into a deep hole in the river. Then he and Sanderson would split up and attack the Japanese from two areas with automatic fire. This did not eventuate but they could hear some movement coming from the area directly opposite them. They finally slept in the open sulap in the company of mosquitoes and ants on the hard bamboo flooring.

The next morning, while using the Boston wireless transmitter to try and contact headquarters with his priority request for food, ammunition, drugs and clothing, Wigzell broke into a transmission. The man on the other end refused to clear the airways. This was too much for Wigzell. In pure New Zealand English he told the man to get the hell off the airwaves and follow the standard procedures for such circumstances. The man on the other end had no choice and cleared the line promptly, as Wigzell and Sanderson were doomed without immediate supplies. This irate episode over the Boston radio was reported to Labuan 'A' Division of 'Z' Special Unit, and when Wigzell returned to base headquarters for debriefing at the end of the war in Borneo he was severely reprimanded.

After completing the 'sked' and getting nowhere, (his request for food and ammunition was again denied) Wigzell and Sanderson decided that their best chance was to try and deceive the Japanese into thinking that an Australian battalion was domiciled at their kampong at Rumah Kadu. The two men put on a great display, drilling an imaginary force in marching and rifle practice, and using their best regimental voices. They hoped that the Japanese would expect a certain degree of opposition if they descended on the Kadu area. During the false regimental display for the Japanese, Wigzell and Sanderson were about 30 metres above the area where the Japanese were situated, and 50 metres inland, so they knew they were safely out of sight.

The Ibans thought the whole situation hilarious, and took great delight in helping by stomping their feet around the kampong square, and trying to imitate Wigzell's and Sanderson's voices.

That night, while they lay in wait for the Japanese, the two men set up two light machine-gun positions along the top side of the longhouse, making sure that their Bren guns were showing, and that the Ibans were on guard. These precautions must have worked, for they were not attacked that night.

Major Toby Carter of Semut 2, their next-door neighbour in the Baram-Brunei River area, heard of their plight and, disregarding all orders from the Australian 9th Division and Allied Intelligence Bureau, despatched two of his own operatives with carriers to Wigzell's base with a plentiful ammunition supply. Fortunately, Carter's men arrived before the Japanese. Two of Wigzell's native guerillas guided them under cover of darkness from the opposite bank of the river, fed them at Rumah Kadu, and then took them downriver and deposited them on a safe track home to their Semut 2 area. The Australian Battalion down at the Ukong still would not assist Wigzell

A Kelabit chief with Major Toby Carter.

and Sanderson in any way, primarily because of the ceasefire and instructions from the 9th Division Headquarters.

The Upper Limbang had not had any rain for many weeks so it would be easy for the Japanese to ford the river upstream without too much effort. The Ibans decided to pray for rain and make a tribal offering to their gods. Wigzell thought himself fortunate that he could witness such an occasion. The longhouse was cleared of everything, and all warlike instruments, including guns, poisoned arrows, sumpitans, knives and anything that could be used to inflict damage, were stacked in the centre of the floor. This area was then declared sacred. All the fighting Ibans, and their elderly people, and Wigzell's and Sanderson's own guerillas sat in a circle around this pile of weapons in the longhouse. Each woman sitting at the rear of her party went to her room or fireplace in the area, filled a coconut shell with arak, which was distilled rice wine, and gave it to the first male in the group. After he drank a small portion, the cup was passed on to the next in line, and so on until the arak was finished. The next woman in the group carried out the same procedure, until everyone present in the room, including Wigzell and Sanderson, had drunk the arak.

Arak is distilled from borak, and has a high alcohol content. The 'Z' men were careful never to drink more than half a glass. The fermenting took place in old dragon jars which had been traded to the natives by the Chinese

Visitors' round sulap at Rumah Kadu. (Drawing by Terri Millar, aged 14.)

traders on the coast hundreds of years previously. The jars were carried from the coast into the interior on the shoulders of the tribesmen from the various kampongs. It was considered to be of great importance to the natives to have as many jars of this native wine as possible, and the more they had, and the older the wine, the higher their rank on the social scale.

The mush from the fermented brew of the borak was fed to the pigs in the kampongs, which made them run about drunkenly. It was one of the pigs' favourite dishes, and they would fight among themselves to see which one could consume the most.

After the native women had given the arak to everybody in the longhouse to drink, a banana palm leaf was made into the shape of a boat with an outrigger and sail. This was filled with fruit and food, and then cast off down the river. Everybody went down to the edge of the river to see the little boat on its way, and Wigzell could not but wonder at the strength of the Ibans' faith.

Twenty-four hours later he was amazed when torrential rain, the heaviest he had encountered in the jungle so far, drenched the little settlement, and continued steadily for two days. The Japanese would not be able to cross the Limbang now.

After another arak session to boost their confidence, Wigzell accompanied 10 Ibans in a perahu downstream, the first time in two weeks that a trip of this sort had been made. As they did not see any Japanese, the men presumed that they had moved further inland.

Further aircraft came into the area and ascertained the position of the Japanese force, which was evidently travelling slowly up the Limbang into the interior. Sanderson went a short distance up the river with his guerilla force and left Wigzell to contact base with an early morning wireless report. On completing this, Wigzell followed Sanderson with his own Kelabits, some local Ibans, and young John, his brave and loyal friend.

Sanderson's trail led towards the Japanese force, and as Wigzell and his men approached this area an excited Iban suddenly ran out of the jungle. He told them that the Japanese were very close, and that he had circled undetected around them. Suddenly, Wigzell realised that Sanderson's perahus, moored on their side of the river, must be protected at all costs. He and his men covered the distance to the river in record time, and for the first time in Borneo, Wigzell took control of a perahu and single-handedly

A parachute supply drop for Semut 1.

crossed the swollen Limbang River. On high ground he then set up his Bren and awaited the return of Sanderson and his men, who arrived an hour later.

The following day, to the joy of the starving men, the British Borneo Civil Administration Unit delivered by Catalina flying boat the first food drop to the guerillas. Their supplies of rice were now completely exhausted, and the food came in the nick of time. There were also tins of Old Gold cigarettes disguised as Planters Peanuts with 50 to the tin. The men had all been smoking native weed rolled in thin banana leaves. Unfortunately, there were no boots or clothing, and a large number of the tins of food were broken and dented and could not be used.

The men's clothes were threadbare, for they had not received any since arriving in the jungle. Harrisson had not even supplied them with mosquito nets or money, and Wigzell felt he had been abandoned and left to fend for himself. From the beginning of his operation in Borneo, he had only two pairs of socks, and one pair of jungle boots, which were wet all the time. The boots had large holes in them and soon fell apart. Perhaps a loin cloth would have sufficed, however, as both men were now considered members of the Limbang Tabon tribe.

It is important to remember that the men had gone back in time when they parachuted into the jungles of Borneo. Other than rice, their staple diet, there was little food, for the Japanese had requisitioned most of the food. And although many areas managed to obtain regular storepedo drops of food, containing many delicacies and extra special comfort parcels, Wigzell and Sanderson were too far from base so they missed out on these.

Further surrender pamphlets were dropped to the Japanese force of Fujino Tai, but still the Japanese did not surrender. They continued to rape, kill, burn and destroy as they retreated. The full surrender had been in force for two weeks since 15 August, and Wigzell and his men were still being sniped at. Two days later, two of the natives were attacked at a local deserted kampong. The following day reports came in from the scout patrol that the main Japanese force were camped on the river bank in sparse jungle 5 km upriver. The scouts reported that these Japanese were completely relaxed, and did not seem to be at all worried about the guerilla force.

The operatives had also just received advice from Semut 2 that Lieutenant Middleton from the Australian forces had advanced through the Tutoh area, and was following the trails of the Japanese. Middleton's instructions were to try and force these Japanese towards the coastline, with the help of Wigzell, Sanderson and their guerillas. Up until now, Wigzell and Sanderson had not actively looked to engage the enemy, although they had been attacked on four occasions. They thought it was time now to show their strength, and with luck they might be able to encourage the Japanese to turn to the west and the coastline, and so come in contact with the Australian 9th Division.

With approximately 100 Ibans and Kelabits, and with young John acting as Bren carrier and ammunition holder, Sanderson and Wigzell, after walking all night, arrived in an area opposite the Japanese camp. They sat down and ate a meal of rice, cooked in coconut juice. The rice was enough to support a man for two days in action. At dawn they moved into position along the bank of the river. This was their advantage, as there was a washout, similar to a trench, made by a previous flood, and the men could lie in this, concealed by the jungle growth overhead.

The camp was full of troops — between 500 and 600 — plus female nurses and camp followers, known as comfort girls, for the troops. Sanderson went upstream to an elevated position so he could observe events, while Wigzell was left to initiate the action.

Wigzell eased the bolt back on his Bren, and let it chatter forward; this was to warn his guerillas of the impending action. He then cocked the Bren and commenced firing, disturbing the cool, calm quietness of the tropical dawn with the thunderous small-arms fire. He emptied 10 magazines during the short period of the action, stopping at times to control the fire of the force, and changing the barrel. The ambush lasted for only about five minutes but the guerillas expended about a thousand rounds in all. The natives had absolutely no fear and laughed and joked with Wigzell all the time. One happy smiling native stood up beside him during the crossfire and indicated the height above his head that a projectile had come singing by.

Perhaps they thought Wigzell needed some encouragement but he had his own motivation. He had recently been told that Ernie Myers — one of the younger New Zealand members of 'Z' who had parachuted into Balikpapan — had been captured and beheaded by the Japanese.

'Bloody murderers,' thought Wigzell. 'This is for young Ernie,' and he let fly.

Sanderson joined Wigzell and called the men out of the trench but as they were about to leave, some Japanese started to climb the trees on the other side of the river to try to locate the operatives' positions.

'Let's give these Nips one more tickle up,' said Wigzell.

Wigzell, John and Iban went back into the trench and sprayed the area where the Japanese were, and abruptly all was chaos again. 'Let's get the hell out of here,' shouted Wigzell to Sanderson over the noise of the crossfire, 'before we're fried by these bastards.' They ran further into the jungle, making for the track leading back to Rumah Kadu.

That night, under cover of darkness, and unbeknown to Wigzell and Sanderson, their Iban warriors crossed the river and inspected the blood-splattered area they had attacked. Japanese dead were everywhere, many of them lying in grotesque positions. They saw one wounded Malay woman, moaning quietly and curled up in the foetal position. She had been left there to die by the Japanese. The Ibans picked her up, carried her to their perahu, and brought her back to Rumah Kadu.

Later that evening, she told Wigzell and Sanderson that many of the enemy had been wounded and killed. Wigzell reported this to base, and was to learn much later that headquarters at Belawit were pleased with this report. However, the top brass considered it to be a breach of the ceasefire order, although the Japanese were still killing, raping and burning as they retreated.

Captain Eric Edmeades, second-in-command of Semut 1, was ordered to enter the area and establish what the situation really was. He went up the river by perahu, but returned after a few hours, saying he had nearly lost his life when the Japanese had machine-gunned his party. He was tipped out of the perahu, luckily near the bank, and lost his rifle, but managed to get safely ashore. He returned downstream as fast as he could to where Wigzell and Sanderson were waiting.

'Christ!' he said. 'I can see what you mean. Those Nips are bloody mad. I was lucky I didn't have my arse shot off back there!'

While Edmeades was talking to Wigzell and Sanderson, the radio suddenly crackled. It was a new station on the air, identifying itself as Labuan Headquarters SRD. There was an urgent message for Wigzell to help the Australian Infantry Forces at Ukong with their radio. The message said: 'A Lieutenant and two perahu-loads of captured Japs are on their way up the Limbang River to try and contact the enemy force moving into the interior. You will advise them to return to base immediately, as this enemy force will be contacted by 'Z' people in the interior.'

This message was received during an electrical storm in the area. He acknowledged the message, and 10 hours later an Australian Lieutenant and two perahu-loads of Japanese appeared on Wigzell's and Sanderson's doorstep. The guerillas had fully armed themselves, as they expected trouble from these Japanese, who were well dressed and well fed. Wigzell gave the message he had received from Labuan Headquarters verbally to the Lieutenant, who immediately asked for this in writing. Otherwise, he said, he would refuse to leave.

Wigzell politely informed the Lieutenant that he was in their area, and written orders did not exist in that part of the world. The Lieutenant glanced at the hostile Ibans, who appeared to be jumpy and waiting for an order from Wigzell. By this time the Japanese in the perahus had started to panic, so the Lieutenant decided he had better leave while his luck was holding.

Shortly after this, Sanderson showed Wigzell a record that their forces in the Limbang had accounted for over 110 enemy killed, as well as many not reported by the natives. This did not include the recent encounter. Small groups of Japanese were pushing through the area all the time, and the two men wondered how long the Japanese could hold out until they were forced to surrender.

Days had turned into weeks since the official end of the war in the Pacific. Wigzell was still unsure if he would ever get out of the jungle alive. He and Sanderson were virtually surrounded by the Japanese, whose forces outweighed their own.

However, on the following day an unexpected development occurred at Rumah Kadu. An excited Iban ran up to Wigzell saying that a Japanese was opposite the kampong waving a pamphlet which had been dropped by the Royal Australian Air Force. The message stated, in Japanese, that the bearer would be given safety and food when surrendering to the Australian forces. As a security measure, Wigzell sent three men in a small perahu across the river to collect the lone Japanese. When the perahu returned with its prisoner, Wigzell and Sanderson tried to obtain as much information as possible from him. This was to little avail, as he did not understand either Malay or English.

That afternoon an intense thunderstorm hit the kampong, and a fireball struck the Boston aerial, blowing out the transmitter. From that point, all efforts to transmit were totally unsuccessful, and Wigzell concluded that the operating crystal and hand generator had been burned out. Two days later, small aircraft arrived overhead, and a new radio set was despatched by storepedo. Unfortunately, the parachute failed to open and everything in the container was destroyed except a note which read: 'Please get on the air again!' This was an impossibility now.

Just before the loss of the radio, Wigzell had signalled the base at Belawit to discontinue their stores, weaponry and ammunition from the interior, as the Fujino Tai Japanese group would probably find them. However, Wigzell's message to the interior supply party was not relayed, as it was out of range. Consequently, Wigzell learned later that the party of men sent in with the stores had been ambushed by the Japanese who, of course, kept the supplies. A guerilla who had served bravely with Sanderson, Usop, was lost in this action.

Lieutenant Middleton from Semut 2 arrived in the area, after following the Japanese through the Tutoh to the Limbang. The Japanese were now trying to encircle Rumah Kadu, and Wigzell and Middleton went downstream to collect a new operative who had been left to assist the natives in the Madalam area. A force of about 40 Japanese were seen trying to cross over the Limbang River on the way through the jungle to their base.

On the way downstream towards the Rumah Badak, which was below the Madalam River, Wigzell and Middleton were attacked by the Japanese, but managed this time to disperse them into the jungle. On the return trip, they were attacked again.

'We've got to knock them off, once and for all,' said Wigzell.

With that, he lifted his US Carbine and commenced pumping shot after shot into the enemy. Out of the corner of his eye, he saw one Japanese up a tree aiming for his head. The bullet whizzed past his ear, wounding him slightly. Without thinking, he automatically fired two shots at the Japanese. As if in slow motion, the Japanese toppled out of the tree, rolling over and over as he hit the ground, blood spurting out like a torrent from his head.

The noise of the battle was deafening; the natives were shouting and screaming, and Wigzell could hear the thump of the jungle parangs as they went in to finish off the killing. With gleeful shouts, the guerillas came rushing out of the jungle holding up the decapitated heads of the unfortunate

Two of the friendly Ibans from the Limbang who came across to Labuan Island SRD headquarters.

Japanese, the bright red blood running in rivulets down the ragged pieces of bone and tissue.

Those Japanese who had managed to escape disappeared and joined the main force who were heading for the interior. They all now headed for the Bawang Valley and Belawit — Wigzell's and Sanderson's headquarters in the interior.

Frank Leckie, from New Zealand, and Paul Bartrum, now Commanding Officer at Belawit headquarters, were preparing at this moment to leave for the Lawas area after collecting arms and ammunition. The war with Japan had been officially over for two months. It was now 13 October.

The Japanese finally surrendered after the arrival of a Japanese envoy from General Baba at Labuan. He carried a letter demanding the immediate cessation of hostilities, which took place on 29 October 1945.

Wigzell was finally ordered out of the Limbang and back to Labuan on 26 September. Sanderson remained in the area to clean up and collect the automatic weapons, leaving a few .303 Lee Enfield rifles and ammunition.

Lt General Masao Baba of the 32nd Japanese Army arrives at Labuan Island to sign the surrender document.

Wigzell was ordered to report to the 2/17th Battalion headquarters at the Ukong River. When he entered the headquarters he was greeted with: 'Oh, another one of those headhunters from up river'.

After months of jungle fighting, he was in no mood to argue with the Australian, and told him he was one of the New Zealanders in the Special Forces of the interior, and did not appreciate being spoken to like that. As the first New Zealander they had come in contact with in Borneo he was treated reasonably well after this.

Instrument of Surrender

In accordance with General Order Number One issued by the Japanese Imperial General Headquarters by direction of the Supreme Commander of the Allied Powers we hereby:—

A. **Proclaim** the Unconditional Surrender to the Commander in Chief, Australian Military Forces of all Japanese Armed Forces and all Armed Forces under Japanese control in the Netherlands East Indies, East of and exclusive of Lombok, and in Borneo.

B. **Command** all Commanders and members of the Japanese Armed Forces and Controlled Forces within the Territories, Islands and Areas aforesaid to cease hostilities immediately, lay down their arms, remain in their present localities and do all such acts and things as may be required of them by the Commander in Chief, Australian Military Forces or his authorised Representative or Representatives.

C. **Command** all Civil, Military and Navy officials and all members of the Japanese Armed Forces to obey and enforce all Proclamations, Orders and Directions issued by the Commander in Chief, Australian Military Forces or his authorised Representative or Representatives.

Signed at Morotai on the Ninth day of September 1945.

Commander Second Japanese Army.
By command and on behalf of Japanese Imperial General Headquarters.

Accepted at Morotai on the Ninth day of September 1945.

T.A. Blamey General
Commander in Chief
Australian Military Forces.

The Surrender Instrument signed at Morotai Island by Lt General Teshima, Commander of the Second Japanese Army, and General Sir Thomas Blamey, Commander of the Australian Imperial Forces.

Wigzell returned next day to Labuan by work boat, having a fresh cooked meal on the way. His stomach was unaccustomed to the high-class food and he was ill straight away. As he had completed three years' active service, he was ordered to return to Australia, and then New Zealand. He arrived back in New Zealand on board an English aircraft carrier just before Christmas 1945, to a joyous welcome from his family. His parents hardly recognised him. His face was gaunt and drawn, and his weight had dropped from 72 kg to 47 kg. He was a young 'old man' of 24.

'My encounter with the natives of Borneo, and all the friends I made there, have given me the greatest experience of my life,' Wigzell says today.

'The knowledge I have gained through working with these wonderful people, their loyalty, and their ability to work together, leaves me with the thought that they could teach outsiders many things.

'Before leaving the Limbang I had my last meal of rice, and I resolved never to touch it again, and for 20-odd years I did exactly that. I gave my trusty old US Carbine, web gear with magazine, ammunition, plus all the army gear I possessed, to John, my friendly young warrior, who gave me his loyalty, and a willingness to be in my company at all times.

'I came into Borneo with nothing, and I went out with nothing.'

Frank Wigzell in recent times with the late Bill Horrocks.

EPILOGUE

As we have seen from Operation Jaywick, one of the first operations of 'Z' Special Unit, 'Z' took some time to establish itself. It was obvious that there was a need for a special-operations unit in the Pacific, as the threat of a Japanese invasion was real. But inevitably, in its early days, mistakes were made.

During the early 1940s the Services Reconnaissance Department faced a daunting task in recruiting and training men from a reluctant military establishment which had little understanding of special operations, and little sympathy for such an unconventional mode of warfare. There was also prejudice from the regular forces, mainly because they were ignorant about the work of SRD. Lieutenant-Colonel Courtney says this was SRD's own fault as they were too secretive. The American General Headquarters regarded them with suspicion and tried to control their activities. It was not uncommon for the Americans to translate the initials of the South-East Asia Command to mean 'Save England's Asiatic Colonies'. In the south-west Pacific area, where General Douglas MacArthur was the supreme Allied commander, similar attitudes to colonialism existed.

The Services Reconnaissance Department, of which 'Z' was the core, inserted 81 parties into Japanese-occupied countries during the Second World War. These missions covered a broad spectrum, from small-scale, specialised, one-night reconnaissance and sabotage raids to the larger inland fighting and intelligence patrols.

Lt Colonel Courtney says the men of SRD had one main advantage over their British interservice counterparts in the Middle East and the United Kingdom — namely, they worked 'together under one Commanding Officer. Elsewhere they were inclined to form their own private armies, which created the problem of competition for men, stores and operational transport, and also the duplication of effort.'

SRD in Sarawak was credited with 1500 Japanese troops killed, and 240 taken prisoner. This was accomplished by approximately 82 officers and men of SRD and approximately 2000 guerillas.

'Z' Special Unit justified its existence by the success of its special operations in Borneo, which helped the assault of the Australian 9th Division and the early defeat of the Japanese forces facing them. The years of trial, error and frustration that went before were the price that was paid by an organisation that started out from scratch, unskilled and unloved.

Courtney says: 'These years produced a high standard of professionalism in the end which contributed significantly, not only to the military result, but to the political stability of the British colonial possessions in the immediate post-war period.'

If a common quality was to be found in all members of 'Z' Special Unit, it would probably be individualism. It seems SOE attracted people who preferred making their own decisions to receiving orders from others. They operated better singly or in small parties rather than in large numbers. It was not enough just to be brave. They had to possess endurance that could take them for days without food or water, an endurance to withstand torture from their enemies, to go without sleep for days on end, and an endurance to believe, above all, in what they were doing. They also needed to be self-disciplined, resourceful and resilient, as is borne out in the stories of Frank Wigzell in Borneo and Don Stott in Greece.

In the years since the end of the Second World War, several prominent historians, including Professor M. R. D. Foot and Kenneth Macksey who have written works on the role of SOE, have concluded that SOE played a vital role and achieved much in the operational field of occupied countries. This was done with a relatively small loss of human life. The same can be said for the special operations carried out in the Pacific by 'Z' Special Unit. It raised and equipped some 6000 guerilla troops in Japanese-occupied territory to provide pre-invasion intelligence and close tactical support for the Australian Infantry Forces.

One must remember too, that the 'Z' operatives were called on to penetrate previously unmapped jungle areas which were peopled by dark-skinned natives, who were often cowed by enemy brutality, and only too eager to collaborate with the enemy for monetary gain. These factors made the acquisition of intelligence difficult, and sometimes impossible.

However, the men had some advantages in that they were fortunate to have no indigenous local government, as in Vietnam, to complicate matters with vested interest, corruption, and political intrigue.

'We were also lucky,' says Lt Colonel Courtney, 'in that the local population in Borneo remained mostly friendly, and the friendship was cemented by a policy of bringing medical treatment to all communities with which SRD operatives were involved.'

I have spent the last three years researching the lives of these men, and I feel

Epilogue

I have come to know them well, one or two perhaps as well as I know myself. The fate of Don Stott, the Lion of Greece, secret agent extraordinary, and one of New Zealand's greatest heroes in every sense of the word, remains a mystery. Did he drown in the storm-whipped seas of Balikpapan Bay, or did he land on the shore and come to a ghastly death at the hands of the Japanese? Unconfirmed reports suggest that this last version could have happened. I hope that this was not so.

One friend of Don's heard after the war that there was evidence that Stott had landed on the shore. Noises of a skirmish with the enemy had been heard and there were signs of a recent battle. However, there has never been any evidence to support this. Bill Horrocks told me that Stott and Leslie McMillan had managed to get to the shore but they had run into the Japanese

The three New Zealand plaques for Don Stott, Robert Houghton and Leslie McMillan at the Labuan Island cemetery at Surrender Point.

who were waiting for them. How did the Japanese know they were coming?

Frank Wigzell and 'Jumbo' Courtney, men who knew the natives of Borneo well, feel sure that this could not have happened. They say that the natives would have been the first to hear of any white men being captured by the Japanese and killed. Nothing could have happened in the jungle without the natives knowing, such was the efficiency of their bush-telegraph service.

A Commission of Enquiry was set up after the war to find out what happened to Stott and McMillan. Some of the natives who were questioned said that a tall, fair-haired man had been seen in the interior of the island, but this was never substantiated.

So what did happen to Stott and McMillan? Although the Commission of Enquiry decided that they had probably drowned while trying to get to the shore, the evidence was by no means conclusive. They were in a light boat, and the night was stormy. If the boat had overturned, the men, weighed down by the heavy equipment and loaded backpacks, would have found it difficult, if not impossible, to stay afloat, or swim to the shore. The Japanese may even have seen them struggling in the water and killed them before they reached land. Also, the seas in Balikpapan Bay are crocodile and shark infested, and the men could have been taken by either of these. The true story may never be known.

Bob Morton went back into Borneo when the war was over to try and find out what happened to his friend, but without success. Bernard Bookman last saw Morton in Auckland one day early in May 1945. He was still wearing his jungle greens, and had just returned to New Zealand from Morotai. He was deeply saddened over the fact that he had been unable to find Stott. Bookman says he had changed from the happy, carefree Morton of earlier days; Stott's death had been a bitter blow. Bookman has wondered many times in the intervening years what became of him.

The other New Zealand member of the Robin 1 party, Bill Horrocks, came back to New Zealand when the war finished, married Barbara, and for a time was editor of *Best Bets*. Afterwards, he set up his own printing company, Horrocks & Sons, and then retired to Canberra. He died there in March 1990.

The heroism and courage of the members of 'Jaywick' and 'Rimau' will long go down in the annals of Australian history, and the tragedy that was Rimau will never be forgotten.

Ivan Lyon's wife, Gabrielle, and son Clive, survived the horrors of Changi Prison, only to be told on their release that Lyon had been killed. French-born Gabrielle never remarried. She and Clive settled in England and

Epilogue

Gabrielle died there some years ago.

What became of the other New Zealand members of the British Military Mission in Greece? Arthur Edmonds of the Royal New Zealand Engineers is still alive and living in Putaruru. Tom Barnes, also of the Royal New Zealand Engineers, and who helped to blow up the Gorgopotamos Viaduct, died in New Zealand some time ago.

Bill Jordan became a Catholic priest after the war, and wrote about his experience in SOE in *Conquest Without Victory*. He died a few years ago.

Charlie Mutch, of the 4th New Zealand Reserve Mechanical Transport and who helped to blow up the Asopos Viaduct, died in Auckland several years ago.

The fearless Frank Wigzell returned to New Zealand and married Marjorie. They have four children and live in Auckland.

The 'most disliked' soldier in all of Borneo, according to the 'Z' operatives, Tom Harrisson, survived the war and stayed on in Borneo. He and his wife died in an accident between a bus and a logging truck while on holiday in Bangkok in 1969.

Five years after Stott went missing, Mary Stott married a Christchurch doctor, Harry Fox, and she and Geoffrey settled in Christchurch. Geoffrey today is married to Sue and they have four children and recently became grandparents.

Members of the Stott family still live in Birkenhead today. Graham Stott, son of Don's brother Hector, was Mayor of Birkenhead for several years. The flamboyant personality and gentle character of Don Stott has touched all their lives in a special way. Barbara Lewis, Don's niece, told me that Don will always be remembered as he was — carefree, impulsive, generous to a fault, warm and loving. Stott — husband, father, son and friend to many — died as he had lived. Chris Woodhouse sums it up perfectly: 'There is not much more that I can add about Don Stott, except that he was the bravest man I ever knew. But that will do.'

The story of Don Stott and the other New Zealanders of 'Z' Special Unit will long be associated with heroism, outstanding courage and dedication. They were the bravest of the brave.

> 'Soldier rest, thy warfare o'er,
> Dream of fighting fields no more.'
>
> SIR WALTER SCOTT, *THE LADY OF THE LAKE*

APPENDIX 1

The names of other New Zealanders who were special service agents in Greece but who have not been mentioned in the book as being part of the British Military Mission to Greece are:

Lt Colonel J. Mulgan, MC (British Army). Died in Cairo, 1945
Lt W. A. Hubbard (Divisional Cavalry). Killed by ELAS guerillas, October 1943
WO2 J. A. Redpath, MM (19 Army Troops Company)
Major J. W. C. Craig, MC & Bar (22 Battalion)
Major A. H. Empson, MM (18 Battalion). Died of sickness in Greece, 6 April 1946
Captain D. G. McNab, MC, DCM (6 Field Company)

APPENDIX 2

NEW ZEALAND ARMY MEMBERS INVOLVED WITH 'Z' SPECIAL UNIT
(COVER NAME 'SPECIAL OPERATIONS AUSTRALIA')

The first party of New Zealanders selected to join 'Z' Special Unit in Australia flew by Teal Sunderland Flying Boat, the 'Aotearoa', flight AW.310 to Sydney on 15 July 1944. This party consisted of eight members, plus the Commanding Officer, Major Don Stott, and two others, who followed at a later date.

Appendices

The 11 members of 'Z' were:

Major Don Stott DSO & Bar (Auckland)
Stott was first a member of the 2 NZ Expeditionary Force and was captured in Crete. He escaped fom a POW camp in Greece and took many months to rejoin his unit in Egypt. He was seconded to SOE and parachuted back into Greece, achieving an almost impossible operation — the destruction of the Asopos Viaduct by using plastic explosives. This delayed German communications by rail for many weeks.
Operation Robin 1 (20 March 1945): Entry into Balikpapan, Borneo, was by submarine, the USS *Perch*. With another New Zealander, Leslie McMillan, was lost, presumed drowned at sea.

Captain Leslie T. McMillan (Auckland)
Operation Robin 1: McMillan was with Major Stott in his folboat which was lost in Balikpapan Bay. Presumed lost at sea by Court of Enquiry at the end of the war.

WO2 Robert G. Houghton (Levin)
Operation Robin 1: Lost in action in Balikpapan during an ambush. Died 26 March 1945.

Captain Bob Morton DCM & MC (Dargaville, Northland)
Member of 2 NZ Expeditionary Force and captured in Crete. Met Major Don Stott while imprisoned in Greece, and both prisoners managed to escape by pole vaulting over the perimeter wire. After returning to his unit in Egypt, Morton joined SOE and parachuted back into Greece for intelligence work with Stott.
Operation Robin 1: Landed in Balikpapan by USS *Perch* after failure of Stott and his party to return to the submarine. Morton took command of the main party, and was subjected to intense Japanese patrol action. He finally escaped to sea after 10 weeks in the jungle. He was awarded the MC for this operation, after receiving the DCM in Greece. Morton went to South Africa after the war, and he is believed to have settled in Greece.

Sergeant Bill Horrocks (Auckland)
Operation Robin 1: Horrocks was originally with the Signals Division in the Pacific and situated in Fiji. He trained in Australia with 'Z' Special Unit, then was sent to Balikpapan, Borneo. Survived 10 weeks in the jungle, and managed to join up with Captain Bob Morton's main party. Escaped to Morotai Allied base.
Died in Canberra 19 March 1990.

Sergeant Graham Greenwood (Christchurch)
Operation Agas 1 (3 March 1945; British North Borneo): Landed in Labuk Bay, North Borneo, on 3 March 1945. The object of the mission was to establish a base on the East Coast of British North Borneo. Landed by submarine, the USS *Tuna*, for the purpose of setting up radio communications with Darwin, gleaning intelligence information from the local natives, and forming native guerilla units in the area. This was a successful mission commanded by Major Chester.
It is not known if Sergeant Greenwood is alive today.

Sergeant W. Sharpe
Operation Agas 1: Not known if alive today.

Corporal Joe Harris (Wellington)
After returning to New Zealand from 2 NZ Expeditionary Force, Harris volunteered as a specialist diesel mechanic for work on 'Z' Special Unit craft in Australia. He overhauled snake craft and Fairmile boats at Garden Island, Western Australia, and Careening Bay. Wounded while extracting faulty round from pistol.
He lives in Wellington.

Sergeant Pat Boyle
Specialist diesel mechanic and work-boat operator in the advanced bases. He did major overhauls on work boats of the 'Z' Special Unit. Finally commanded the 'Black Snake' in the forward base at Morotai and Labuan islands, landing operatives and supplies in enemy-held areas.
Died Wellington, 11 October 1976.

Sergeant Richard J. Newlick
Specialist diesel mechanic. Trained and worked in Australia on diesel craft of 'Z'. He now lives near Opotiki.

WO2 Louis N. Northover
Operated with the British Expeditionary Force and the Allied Military Mission in Greece from 1941. Trained and worked on diesel craft in Australia. Seconded to 'Z' in Australian 12 July 1945. Died Auckland 22 September 1981.

The second party to join 'Z' Special Unit departed from New Zealand by the USS freighter *Waipouri* in December 1944. This party, known as Robin 2, had eight members:

Lt Frank Leckie (Christchurch)
Stallion 5: Weston, Sipitang, Brunei Bay, Borneo; June 1945.
Stallion 8: Palau Saat, Brunei Bay, Borneo; 13-14 June 1945. The purpose of this mission was to record intelligence information.
Semut 1: Entry by work boat at Lawas after landing by Australian Infantry Forces, then into the interior of Sarawak (Dutch and British North Borneo), 25 March 1945. One of the last of the 'Z' men to vacate the area, and helped to take the last surrender of Japanese in Borneo in the Bawang area.
Died Christchurch 1977.

Lt Bob Tapper (now living at Pukekohe)
Platypus 2: Successful in removing natives from sea-going perahus in the Balikpapan area for interrogation, and later selected well-informed natives from Balikpapan for intelligence information at Morotai headquarters.
Platypus 3: Deceived the enemy by focusing attention on the area north-east of Balikpapan. This was done by the natives passing rumours through the jungle, by flying over the particular area at low altitude as if on a reconnaissance mission, and by dropping a marked map of operational instructions, together with beach marks on the beach near Senipan where it would be picked up. The success of the mission was proved when large native patrols were sighted in the area.
Playtypus 4: The extraction of 18 informants from Balikpapan and distribution of rumours as in above.
Platypus 11: Semoi, Mentawir, and Sepakos areas. This was to obtain information about POWs in the district. Reliable native informers made it possible for the recovery of 63 Indian prisoners.

Signalman Ernie Myers (Invercargill)
Platypus 7: Parachute insertion into Balikpapan, Semoi and Mt Mentawir for intelligence purposes (21 km west of Balikpapan). The dropping area had not been checked but the men were still parachuted into this area, and consequently the mission failed. This was Ernie Myers' first parachute drop. Three of the operatives landed in a Japanese camp area, and although they fought their way out, causing many casualties in the process, they were finally captured. Ernie Myers and Malay Sergeant Ma'eroff Bin Said were tortured and killed, probably on 30 June 1945.
New Zealander Bob Tapper, who worked with the War Graves

Commission immediately after the surrender of the Japanese, recovered the two bodies from their graves, and now they are interred in the War Graves Cemetery on Labuan Island, Brunei Bay, Borneo. The Japanese responsible were tried and executed by the War Crimes Tribunal.

Signalman Allen Campbell (Stoke, now living in Australia)
Broke his leg on the parachute course at Richmond, New South Wales. He did not take part in any 'Z' operations.

Corporal George Edlin (Invercargill)
Swift: North-west Halmaheras, Race Island — intelligence information, May 1945.
Stallion 8: Palau Saat, Brunei Bay, Borneo. To report on enemy radar installations. Edlin was also radio operator on one of 'Z's Fairmile work boats, supplying operatives with requirements in occupied Borneo.
Semut 1: After the 9th Australian Division had landed in Borneo, Edlin worked the wireless 'Z' connection from Lawas on the mainland, then went into the ULU of Sarawak. Returned to New Zealand on Labour Day 1945 on the hospital ship *Andes* with Captain Bob Morton.
Alive today.

Sergeant Jack Butt (Auckland)
Stallion 5: Weston, Sipitang, Brunei Bay, Borneo. For intelligence information, under party leader Lt Frank Leckie.
Stallion 8: Palau Saat, Brunei Bay, Borneo. To record intelligence information — party leader Lt Frank Leckie.
Semut 1: Entry into Borneo via Lawas and work boat, after 9th Australian Division landing at Borneo, then into Sarawak and British North Borneo with Lt Frank Leckie.
Died in Auckland.

Signalman Neil Fleming
Stallion 5: Weston, Sipitang, Brunei Bay, Borneo. Under party leader Lt Frank Leckie.
Stallion 8: Palau Saat, Brunei Bay, Borneo. To record intelligence information.
Platypus 9: Balikpapan; July 1945. Proceeded to a northern point where radio communications were set up with Morotai Island SRD headquarters to report on enemy activity in the area.

Sergeant Frank Wigzell (Auckland)
Semut 1: Main operation inside Borneo. Parachuted in the interior of

Sarawak, and landed just over the border in the then Dutch area, Bawang Valley, Belawit.

Sergeant Ross Shakes (RNZAF, Auckland)
Enlisted in the RNZAF as a radio mechanic with previous experience. Following training at Wigram, he was sent to the United Kingdom on attachment to the RAF for advanced training in radar. Posted to an operational radar station in East Fife, from where he was recruited in May 1942 by the Special Operations Executive, London, as a radio communications specialist. Volunteered for service abroad, arriving at Meerut, north of Delhi, December 1942. Served with ME9, ME25 and force 136 SEAC. These units were controlled by SOE London as part of its worldwide operational intelligence activities. Following furlough leave in New Zealand he travelled to Melbourne on the *Akaroa*, being seconded to 'Z' Special Unit, SRD. Was flown to Morotai in the Halmaheras, then to Zamboanga and Tarakan to the advance base of Labuan Island, Brunei Bay, Borneo, which was captured by the Australian 9th Division on June 10 1945. His responsibilities at this location were to maintain technical lines of communication with the operatives of 'Z' in the interior of British North Borneo and Sarawak until all Japanese resistance ceased after the surrender document was signed.

Two other New Zealanders served with 'Z' Special Unit, but they enlisted as British and Australian Army members. They played a prominent part in the British Northern Borneo and Sarawak theatre of operations. They were:

Major G. S. (Toby) Carter DSO (Rotorua)
Lt Eric Edmeades (Adelaide, Australia)

APPENDIX 3

SPECIAL OPERATIONS AUSTRALIA
'Z' SPECIAL UNIT

Total personnel at the end of the war	1704
Operatives trained	550
Operatives who saw action	380
Total number parachuted into operation areas	78
Australians in force	1250

(Included in the above were 59 female members, who acted as wireless operators and cipher personnel in Australia)

Decorations received by unit	150
Casualties (including 2 Malay personnel)	81

(Figures for Flight 200 RAAF Liberators are not included in the above totals.)

Operatives from the following countries participated in 'Z' Special Unit: Australia, Great Britain, Canada, Holland, New Zealand, China, Malaya, USA.

Areas of operation: Singapore, Malaya, Timor, Java Sea, China Sea, Borneo, Philippines, New Guinea, New Hebrides.

APPENDIX 4

The Semut 1 operation in Borneo was considered the most successful of all the operations in the Pacific by 'Z' Special Unit. At the height of this operation, operatives and local guerillas controlled an area of 10 000 square km, containing 125 000 people. The force consisted of the following:

Australian AIF	34
NZ Expeditionary Force	4
British Expeditionary Force	3
Royal Australian Air Force	1
Total	42

Semut 1 accounted for the following enemy casualties and prisoners:

Killed	1001
Taken prisoner	35
Auxiliaries killed	32
Aux/Coolies taken prisoner	201
Total	1269

Semut 1 casualties:

Whites killed	nil
Muruts killed	12
Tagals killed	4
Ibans killed	4
Chinese killed	1
Total	21

(32 operatives were dropped by parachute)

APPENDIX 5

Operational orders from Major Tom Harrisson, O/C Semut 1, for Lt J. Westley AIF on arrival in the interior of Borneo by parachute to join the party — 3 June 1945.

ORDERS FOR BAHAU RIVER AND TANJONG SELOR AREA

At this moment all rice from the TAANJONG SELOR Area is being sent by perahu to 'BROUGINE' on the BAHU RIVER, rice from MACASSER is also arriving at BROUGINE BY STEAMER and a distribution to Japanese forces is being made from there.

1. YOU WILL STOP THE WHOLE OF THE RICE TRAFFIC IN THAT AREA. You will take all possible precautions against hostile natives as there are many of them in that area.
2. You will make a census of all villages called at whether hostile or otherwise, this will assist the Government in times of peace as most of the country you will be travelling in has not yet been visited by white men.
3. You will have all tracks you travel over improved by the natives as a voluntary village service. Be firm on this point.
4. You will keep a diary of your movements as well as a track log and times of travel from place to place, detailed maps will be made out from these and sent back here to Head Quarters periodically.
5. You will go to LONG POENDJOEGAN and KILL all the remaining Japanese there, number there at the moment unknown, maybe twenty odd.
6. You will kill or capture the Government Official 'KIAI HERON' if able to capture bring back here to Head Quarters.
7. You will go to LONG BERINI on the BAHAU RIVER and KILL the 'GOORU' there, he is a strong JAP sympathiser and is assisting them wholeheartedly.
8. No food will be sent with you as we have none to spare you must live off the land. You will find it hard as reports indicate that the Japs have conscripted all foods for their own use.
9. Do not molest the women and pay full attention to native goodwill as

our lives in this country depend very much upon it, no shooting up of hostile campongs except as a last resort or unless PROGRESS IS HALTED.

10. Route will be — Loemboedeat-Pa Kurid-Pa Oopan-Pa Ibung-then jungle to Long Toea-Long Berini-Long Poendjoegan, approximately a fifteen day trip. On arrival Long Toea you will be in unknown territory and it is up to you from there on.
11. You will prepare a system of runners so that a message of progress can be sent back to me every five days AND SEE THAT THEY DO GET BACK, your maps reports and intelligence is of the utmost importance to Corps H.Q. AND TO THE OUTSIDE WORLD.
12. Bring back all documents etc taken from the Japanese bring back all colaborators and Informants, capture and bring back all Malays.
13. Propagander all villages encountered and bring back all likely guerilla recruits.
14. On the way back, go to PUN on the River PUN and find out who killed TUAN HUDDIN. Capture and bring back the 'KAPALA' be particularly careful — one hundred percent hostile campong.
15. Look out for likely Dropping Zones both for live drops and stores drops, find also a place where a Catalina can land and take off, preferably on the KAYAN or BAHU Rivers.
16. You will take ten guerillas only, comprising five Malays and five Dyaks. One Bren gun . . . six grenades . . . three sub-machine-guns . . . six 303 Rifles and plenty of ammunition.
17. If all goes well you should be back here one month from now, if you are in trouble do not repeat do not send for help as all personnel will be occupied elsewhere. If upon your return here you find we have been killed captured or driven out you must get out the best way you can preferably to TARAKAN as there are huge Jap forces to the North of us the south of us and to the East of us but as far as we can ascertain not near as many to the West of us, except on and around TARAKAN.

This constitutes your orders, they are very brief but most Yours is a difficult and dangerous assignment and one moment day or night (if you hope to survive) must you forget vigilence. Remember you are in two enemy territories Japs and natives both.

DO NOT repeat DO NOT get yourself killed as there are too few of us here as it is.

GOOD HUNTING GOODLUCK AND GOODBYE

A. I.

APPENDIX 6

LETTERS AND REPORTS

Letter from Frank Leckie to Jeff Westley (AIF)

HQ BIF 12.11.45
(Borneo Interior Force)
Belawit

Dear Jeff,

Still doing business at the same old stand, as you can see by the address. Made a leisurely trip back after leaving you and arrived to find the place deserted, except for Ray Bennett and Paul (Bartrum) who were leaving the next day. So I tagged along as well, but we only got as far as Ba Kelalan, when Sualong and his soldiers told us there were about 400 Nips at Long Beluyu, and they were not too friendly towards the natives. This was not the mob that Sandy and Frank had a go at on the Limbang, and did over 55 of them.

They fired on the natives at Long Beluyu, but got rather the worst of the argument as the natives replied, and killed 5 of them. We promptly headed for the Bawang again, but as there was nothing doing, I went back to Ba Kelalan. The next day news came that they were coming our way so we prepared to have a bit of fun. The natives all shot through when the Nips left Long Beluyu but I managed to rally them a little, and then Paul arrived to have a look at things. We organised a nice little ambush for them and they stopped at Pala that day. Next day, Paul, who was itching for a chance to get stuck into some Japs after so much administration work, sent me to organise the evacuation of Belawit. The Nips duly arrived that day and very obligingly walked into the ambush. Sualong did some marvellous work with the Bren, and we found out later about 30 Nips were killed. They retired in rather a hurry to think things over, then they sprung a surprise and attacked at night.

In the meantime the Boss (Harrisson) had left Lawas with two Jap envoys to contact the Japs and try to get them to surrender. They had a hell of a trip owing to floods, and it was only the fact that we delayed the Japs a couple of days that allowed them to catch up. Anyway the envoys finally persuaded the 2 I/C, Kamimura, to give in. Thank the Lord for that as I had visions of chasing around Borneo again for a few more months as a guerilla once more.

The Japs started off 578 strong and finished up 358, including 5 women and 1 child — plenty of medical stores, 2 doctors, 1 Chinese nurse and all the arms in the world — mortars, grenades, mostly Aussie ones, pistols, swords (60), and over 200 rifles. So altogether it was a lucky break for us that they turned it in. We lost 2 killed and 2 wounded. Not bad for over 30 Japs. What with Sandi's 55 in the Limbang, SRD had its fair share of the party, while 9th Division did exactly . . . towards it.

It looks very much as though I'll be very lucky to reach Australia before Xmas now, as I'm leaving tomorrow to go out via Long Berang and Malinau. Have to pay off all those soldiers and coolies of yours in that area. The Boss went horribly crook at SRD for clearing all personnel out before he had a chance to arrange things such as payment, etc.

So I'll say cheerio for now, Jeff, and hope to run across you one of these days. All the very best for Xmas and the New Year, and I hope you arrive home in time for it. Wish me luck too, will you?

Frank

August 1, 1945

From: 9TH DIV. AT UKONG
2/17 Battalion message.
SGT SANDERSON

CO has visited here. He instructs as follows:
We are under a qualified cease fire order, and he will not send men or ammunition. I am sending the last of your ammunition — we have an ample supply here. Asked that you keep us posted with facts as to Jap movements and any reports as to his apparent intentions. When you draw conclusions from anything you see, could you support them with details of your observation? At the moment we are not to make active steps to stop the Jap, and all efforts are being made to produce proof of surrender. So suggest that you, rather than taking active action against him, maintain close watch on his movements and keep us well posted. You will see it is preferred that the Jap be kept in his large body, rather than broken into small groups.

This aspect may be hard to explain to the natives — it is their food which is being pilfered, but there it is.

If you or your force are seriously threatened, you should withdraw in this direction. Keep in mind the object required — that is to closely observe the enemy's movement and keep us well informed.

Dyaks report that there has been more war between you and the Japs. Hope it is not too serious.

The following is part of a special report on the Limbang from Semut 2:

TOP SECRET
PATROL REPORT MELINAU-LIMBANG AREA
BY LIEUTENANT P. V. MIDDLETON
6 October 1945

Along the entire route over the watershed and down to Rumah Badek the only Japanese dead we saw were four who had been left to die along the track and two who had been hung.

I sent seven carriers and two scouts back to Melinau River as they were no longer required.

I contacted Sergeant Sanderson at Rumah Kadu and at his suggestion, split my force — Corporals Graham and McLean with four soldiers were left at Rumah Badek and the remainder moved upstream to Rumah Kadu where the wireless was.

Sergeant Sanderson was in command of this area so I took over from him and signalled F/L Bartrum to that effect. A holding force at Rumah Bilong 20 minutes up stream was reinforced by Sergeant Gilman and one native soldier.

The two whites had been in this area for 6 weeks and had NOT been supplied with rations, clothing or ammunition.

On or about the 19 September BBCAU had sent in a supply to be free dropped. Approximately 60 percent of these stores were lost owing to breakages etc. On 22 September a drop of 1 Wireless set, a small supply of rations and trade stores came in. Frequent signals from me to Labuan failed to produce further stores. We existed on native food and surplus rations sent to us by Division troops at Ukong. Ammo supply was almost exhausted and could not be replenished. During a 'sked' Bartrum notified us that a carrying party sent by him to Sergeant Sanderson and carrying 30 rifles, 5 SMGs and 3 tins of first aid had been ambushed at Madahit and everything lost. Trying to supply Sergeant Sanderson from Belawit and right through the Jap lines, is in my opinion contrary to the most elementary principles of warfare.

The impression I gained was that the original force in the Limbang (Sanderson and Wigzell) had been criminally neglected, left to fend for themselves and expected to do almost impossible things, and were not supplied with money.

Actions

September 22 — Sergeant Sanderson went 3 hours upstream to recce that area. Previously this house had been used as a sort of staging camp for the Japs. Investigations showed that a party of approximately 40 had crossed the Limbang River, and according to native reports, were making for Rumah Kadu. They would take three days to reach Kadu.

September 25 — Sergeant Wigzell and myself went downstream to bring Corporal Graham back to reinforce HQ at Rumah Kadu. Outside Rumah Lasong which is between Kadu and Badak, the natives informed us that there were 30 Japs on the opposite bank. These appeared to be completing the encirclement of Kadu. Shots were exchanged after which the Japs withdrew.

After picking up Corporal Graham we were moving upstream when the Japs opened up again. At the time the perahu was in shallow water so we got out and on to a small island and engaged the enemy. After this action I saw that Corporal Graham had been hit on the hand, while being attacked with grenades launched from dischargers.

Further upstream we were attacked again, making 3 times in one day. We reasonably suspected that we had killed 5 enemy.

26 September Patrolling the entire area failed to locate any Japs, but warm fires showed where they had been.

27 September Taking one day's rations, my party started to return to Marudi, as instructed by Major Wilson.

(Signed) P. V. Middleton — Lieut

A letter from Lt Jeff Westley (AIF) of the first reinforcement to Semut 1 Operation, to Sergeant Frank Wigzell. It is included here to illustrate the degree of trust and respect that could exist between soldiers and natives in Borneo.

20 June 1989

Selamat Tinggal Saya Punya Kawan Frank,
You mentioned how well you and Sandy got on with the Dayaks and Ibans. I can understand that as I spent time with every tribe in Borneo, including the treacherous Tagals of British North Borneo, and with them you could expect a dart in the back at any time, day or night. Boy, did I lose some sleep, until one day I heard a story from a wizened-up old senile warrior. He told me that in the old days it was possible to be made a blood brother of a tribe under certain circumstances, and that if one were accepted, he would never be betrayed. This is just what I wanted, and I asked him if he could arrange it. He said he would talk to the reigning elders, and stated that gifts would have to be exchanged. He also enquired if I had anything to offer. I replied gold. (Sovereigns minted in 1942 were to pay our guerillas, as paper money was not acceptable after Japanese occupational currency.)

Three days later it was arranged. I had to go to a small longhouse half a day's walk away. I was allowed my weapons, including 6 grenades. Five 'Kiais', or learned tribespeople of the area, were seated in a circle facing inwards, surrounded by a circle of some 30 decorated braves, standing and facing inwards also. No weapons were in sight. On the mat in the centre of the ring was a knife from a parang pouch — a cup made from two-thirds of a coconut shell. It looked ancient. Room was made for me in the inner circle. Nervously I looked outside to make sure that I was visible to my guerillas stationed there, for they had their orders. The elder of the Kiais took charge — picked up the knife and nicked his wrist, and pressed his thumb on the cut. The others did the same. I picked up the knife, looked at the Kiai and then my wrist. He nodded so I followed the pattern. On picking up the coconut shell he placed it in front of me then held his wrist to mine for about half a minute. A small amount of both our blood oozed out and dropped into the shell cup. The other Kiai's followed the same ritual.

Next the head Kiai nicked my ear lobe and held the shell under it, blood spurting into it. The same was done to all the standing warriors. The shell cup was now taken over to a huge jar, and a gourd full of its contents transferred into it, (arak, I believe). It was then handed to me with the sign to drink. I drank. The Kiais drank, then the warriors. Everyone began talking excitedly, and I never understood a word.

My guerillas were called into the longhouse, and everyone began a session on the borak and arak. Food was also provided. I was presented with some beautiful bead-work — a century old, at least, three panels in all. I have never seen anything to equal this in Borneo during the rest of my travels. In return I presented each of the Kiais with a gold sovereign, and I carved Semut 1 on the King's Head with their still-bloody knife. It went over real big. From then on I had no further trouble with the Tagals.

The moment we entered one of their villages, I had it spread around that I was a blood brother of their tribe, telling them in detail of the grisly ceremony, and knowing the natives as you do, you can imagine some of the stories that circulated. One thing I learned — never, never, hit a Tagal. Kill him, yes, but hit him, and you have an enemy for life. One day he will get you — you can depend on it — brother or not.

Best wishes.
Jeff.

BIBLIOGRAPHY

Beevor, J. G. *SOE — Recollections and Reflections 1940-45,* The Bodley Head, 1981.
Byford-Jones, W. *Greek Trilogy.* Hutchinson, 1945.
Churchill, Winston S. *The Second World War* Volume III; *The Greek Campaign,* Cassell, 1950.
Courtney, G. B. (unpublished manuscript).
Cruickshank, Charles. *SOE in the Far East,* Oxford University Press, 1983.
Davidson, Basil. *Special Operations Europe,* Victor Gollancz, 1981.
Davin, D. M. *Official N.Z. War History — Crete,* War History Branch, 1953.
Elliott, Murray. *Vasili — The Lion of Crete,* Century Hutchinson, 1987.
Eudes, Dominique. *The Kapetanios: Partisans and Civil War in Greece 1943-49* (tr. from French by John Howe), N.L.B., 1972.
Farran, Roy. *Winged Dagger,* Collins, 1948.
Foot, M. D. R. *SOE 1940-45,* Mandarin, 1990.
Foot, M. D. R. *SOE In France: An Account of the British Special Operations Executive in France 1940-44,* HMSO, 1966.
Hall, D. O. W. *The Prisoners of Italy,* War History Branch, 1949.
— *The Prisoners of Germany,* War History Branch, 1949.
— *The Prisoners of Japan,* War History Branch, 1949.
Harrisson, Tom. *The World Within,* Cresset Press, 1959.
Heckstall-Smith, Anthony and Baillie-Grohman, Vice-Admiral. *Greek Tragedy,* Anthony Blond Ltd, 1961.
History of the Second World War, Purnell & Sons Ltd, London, 1966.
Howarth, Patrick. *Undercover,* Arrow Books, 1980.
Jordan, William. *Conquest Without Victory,* Hodder & Stoughton, 1969.
Kiriakopoulos, G. C. *Ten Days to Destiny,* Franklin Watts, 1985.
Ladd, James. *Commandos & Rangers of World War 2,* Redwood Burn, 1978.
Lawrence, T. E. *Seven Pillars of Wisdom,* Jonathan Cape, 1935.
Long, Bob. *'Z' Special Unit's Secret War: Operation Semut 1,* 1989.
McClymont, W. G. *To Greece — Official History,* Whitcombe & Tombs, 1959.
McGlynn, M. B. *Special Service in Greece,* War History Branch.
McKie, Ronald. *The Heroes,* Angus & Robertson, 1960.

Marshall, Bruce. *The White Rabbit: The Story of Wing Commander F. F. E. Yeo-Thomas*, Evans, 1952.
Mentiplay, Cedric. *A Fighting Quality*, A. H. & A. W. Reed, 1979.
Minney, R. D. J. *Carve Her Name With Pride — The Story of Violette Szabo*, Collins, 1964.
Moss, W. Stanley. *Ill Met By Moonlight*, Harrap, 1950.
Mulgan, John. *Report On Experience*, Oxford University Press, 1947.
Myers, E. C. W. *Greek Entanglement*, Rupert Hart-Davies, 1955.
Saraphis, S. *Greek Resistance Army: The Story of ELAS*, Birch Books, 1951.
Spencer-Chapman, F. *The Jungle is Neutral*, Chatto & Windus, 1952.
Strabolgi, R. N., Lord. *Singapore & After*, Hutchinson, 1942.
Tickell, Jerrard. *Odette: The Story of a British Agent*, Chapman & Hall, 1949.
Trenowden, Ian. *Operations Most Secret SOE: The Malayan Theatre*, William Kimber & Co., 1978.
Turner, Don. *Kiriakos: A British Partisan in Wartime Greece*, W. H. Allen & Co., 1982.
Woodhouse, C. M. *Apple of Discord*, Hutchinson, 1948.
— *The Struggle for Greece 1941-49*, Rupert Hart-Davis, McGibbon, 1976.
— *Something Ventured*, Granada, 1982.

INDEX

Allied Intelligence Bureau (AIB) 83, 85, 86, 88, 131
Alamein Line 11, 12, 14
'Animals' (Operation) 30
Ares, Veloukhiotis 3, 22, 24, 25, 26
Asopos viii, 14, 28, 34, 35, 36, 147, 148
Athens 6, 8, 9, 10, 14, 15, 28, 30, 31, 36, 37, 38, 39, 41, 45
Australian 9th Division 106, 123, 127, 130, 131, 132, 136, 143, 152, 153, 159

Baba, Masao General 107, 140
Ba Kelalan 109, 158
Balikpapan viii, xv, 50, 51, 59, 60, 65, 97, 98, 136, 145, 146, 149, 151, 152
Barker, Nat 21
Barnes, Tom vii, 3, 147
Bartrum, Paul 140, 158, 160
Belawit 91, 102, 104, 105, 109, 118, 121, 124, 137, 138, 140, 152, 158, 160
Berryman, M. M. 72, 76
Bin Ali 50, 62, 63, 64, 65
Blamey, Sir Thomas 70, 78, 86
Bookman, Bernard 10, 17, 146
Borneo vii-viii, ix, xvi, 46, 48-50, 73, 76, 77, 82, 84, 88-90, 92, 96, 97-99, 101, 102, 104, 107, 108, 110, 116-22, 126, 131, 134, 135, 142-44, 151-56, 162, 163
Boyle, Pat 150
British Military Mission (BMM) vii, 3, 4, 15, 18, 22, 24, 28, 35, 44, 148, 150
British North Borneo 57, 151, 162
Brunei 90, 106, 108, 116, 151, 152, 153
Butt, Jack 113, 152

Cain, K. P. 72, 76
Cairo viii, 10, 11, 12, 15, 18, 21, 26, 28, 30, 36, 37, 42, 43, 44
Campbell, Allen 152
Carey, W. C. 79
Carse, H. E. (Ted) 70, 72, 73, 76
Carter, Toby 89, 90, 119, 131, 153
Changi 69, 74, 146
Churchill, Sir Winston S. 3, 18, 85
Corinth 42, 45
Cotterill, Harry 48

Courtney, Lt-Col. G. B. (Jumbo) 57, 76, 78, 143, 144, 146
Craig, J. W. C. 148
Crete 3, 6, 8, 11, 14, 148, 149
Crilley, A. 72, 76

Da Roza, Joe 111
Davidson, D. M. N. 72, 73, 75, 78, 79
Desphina 36, 38, 81
Dey, R. L. 50, 60, 61, 62
Dooland, Bruce xvi, 50, 51, 52, 58, 59, 60, 62, 63, 64
Dua, Kondoy 50, 61, 62
Dwyer, Bill 50, 59, 60-63, 65, 66

EAM 28, 42
Edes 3, 22
Edlin, George 95, 113, 117, 119, 152
Edmeades, Eric 137, 153
Edmonds, Lt-Col. Arthur vii, 3, 28, 31, 32, 34, 147
Elas 3, 22, 26, 28, 43, 148
Empson, A. H. 148
Eudes, Dominique 43, 44

Falls, W. G. 72, 73, 75, 79, 84
Farquharson, L. 50, 61, 62, 65
Fleming, Neil 152
Foot, M. R. D. 144
Fox, Mary see Stott, Mary
Frazer Island 86, 95, 96, 110, 113
Fujino Tai 129, 130, 135, 138

Georgatos, Angelos 39, 40, 41
Gordon-Creed, Geoffrey 15, 18, 19, 24, 26, 27, 28, 29, 30-34, 50
Gorgopotamos Viaduct 3, 14, 147
Greece vii-viii, 3, 4-8, 10-15, 18, 19, 21, 22, 24, 26, 28, 35, 43-45, 145, 147, 148-50
Greenwood, Graham 150
Griffiths, Bob 90
Griffiths-Marsh, Roland 128

Harris, Joe 150
Harrisson, Tom 89, 90, 98, 99, 101, 102, 104, 110, 115-19, 121, 122, 130, 135, 147, 156, 158

Index

Hinton, Jack 8
Horrocks, Bill ix, xv-xvi, 50-52, 58-60, 62-64, 145, 146, 149
Houghton, Robert 50, 61, 62, 149
Hubbard, W. A. 148
Huston, A. W. 72, 73, 75, 79, 81

Jaywick, Operation 57, Chapter 6, 77-79, 84, 143, 146
John (Wigzell's guide) 111-13, 119, 120, 122, 134, 136, 142
Jones, A. M. W. 72, 73, 75
Jordan, Bill viii, 13, 14, 15, 147

Karadjopoulos, George 29
Keble, Brigadier C. M. 43
Khouri 31, 34
Kofuku Maru see *Krait*
Krait 57, 69, 70, 71, 72, 73, 75, 76, 77
Kuala Madalam 127

Labuan 76, 118, 131, 137, 140, 142, 150, 153
Lawas 106, 110, 115, 117, 152, 158
Leckie, Frank 97, 113, 117, 140, 151, 152, 158
Lewis, Barbara 46, 147
Limbang 106, 117, 119, 120-23, 126, 127, 130, 132, 133, 135, 137, 138, 140, 142, 158, 160, 161
Lloyd, Ian 104, 106, 107
Lockwood, Chester 29
Long, Bob 90, 102, 105, 118
Long Miau 104, 106, 107, 108
Loss, Colonel 40, 41, 43, 44
Lyon, Clive 69, 146
Lyon, Gabrielle 69, 73, 74, 75, 146, 147
Lyon, Lt-Col. Ivan 57, 69, 70, 72, 73, 77, 78, 79, 80, 81, 146

MacArthur, General Douglas 86, 143
McDowell, J. P. 72, 73, 75
McIntyre, Harry 28, 29, 31, 32, 34, 38, 39
McKie, Ronald 67, 78, 80
Macksey, Kenneth 144
McMillan, Leslie xvi, 48, 50, 51, 52, 58, 60, 62, 65, 145, 146, 149
McNab, D. G. 148
McPherson, Colin 104, 107
Marinos, Captain Themi 22
Marsh, E. W. 72, 76
Meehan, Edna 47
Middleton, Lt P. V. 135, 138, 139, 160, 161
Morotai viii, 65, 86, 88, 89, 91, 97-99, 113, 146, 149, 150-53
Morris, R. G. 72, 76
Morton, Captain Robert M. ix, xv-xvi, 6-18, 27-31, 36-40, 47-52, 59-62, 65, 66, 146, 149, 152
MSC 71, 77, 78, 80

Mulgan, John 21, 26, 148
Mustika 79, 80
Mutch, Charlie 31, 34, 36, 147
Myers, Brigadier E. C. W. vii-viii, 3, 4, 15, 18, 21, 22, 24, 26, 28, 29, 34, 35, 43, 44
Myers, Ernest 136, 151

Neubacher, Hermann 40, 43
Newlick, Richard J. 150
Nibbs, Bill 99, 111, 115, 116
Nikiphoros, Dimitriou 26
Northover, Louis N. 150

Pa Berayong 110-12, 115, 117, 119
Pa Brunot 117, 119, 124
Padas 104, 108
Page, R. C. 72-75, 78, 79, 84
Papagos, General 44
Pa Pala 104, 105, 106
Parnassus 24, 36
Perch xv-xvi, 50, 58, 59, 149
Pinkerton, Lt Bob 110
Piraeus 14
Porpoise HM 79, 82
Psaros, Demetrios 22, 24, 26, 27, 28

Ranu (Wigzell's guide) 119, 120, 122
Redpath, A. 148
Reynolds, Bill 69
Richter, Gordon 104
Rimau, Operation 57, Chapter 7, 146
Robin 1 & 2, Operation 50, 57, 58, 60, 97, 98, 149
Rommel, Field-Marshal Erwin viii, 15, 18
Roumeli 3, 14, 15, 18, 148
Rumah Kadu 123, 126, 127, 131, 136-39, 160, 161

Sanderson, Fred ix, 89, 106, 117, 119, 121, 123, 125-28, 130-33, 134-36, 138, 140, 158, 159, 160, 161, 162
Sarawak 89, 90, 98, 104, 108-10, 117, 120-23, 143, 151-53
Satu, Kondoy 50, 61, 62
Schumann, Haiz 39, 40, 41, 42
Scott, Kenneth 28, 29, 31, 32, 34
Semut, Operation 88-91, 98, 101, 102, 115, 117, 119, 131, 135, 137, 138, 152, 154, 156, 162
Shakes, Ross 153
Sharpe, W. 150
Sicily 30, 35, 37
Simcock, Dr Keith 47
Singapore viii, 57, 67, 69-71, 73-75, 77-80, 82-86, 154
SOA 86, 116, 154
SOE vii, 3, 13, 18, 43, 57, 76, 77, 85, 86, 87, 88, 89, 94, 144, 147-49, 153

SRD 49, 57, 78, 79, 80, 82, 83, 86, 87, 88, 117, 137, 143, 144, 152, 159
Sterling, Bill 16
Stevens, John 13, 15
Stott, Bob 5, 48
Stott, Major Donald J.: early life 4-6; capture in Crete 6; escape from POW camp 8; disguised as a Greek 8-10; and Bob Morton ix, xv, 6-9, 11-17, 27-30, 36, 38, 40-42, 49-52; first work with SOE 11-17; in Cairo 10-13; parachute training 13-14; first operation in Greece 18-20; Asopos sabotage 28-35; peace talks with Germans viii, 39-42; return to New Zealand 46; military decorations vii, 34, 46; marriage 47; training in Australia 48-50; insertion into Borneo 50; disappearance and death xv-xvi, 52, 60, 62, 66, 144-46, 148 *see also* Robin 1
Stott, Ethel 5
Stott, Geoffrey 49, 147
Stott, Graham 147
Stott, Hector 147
Stott, John 48
Stott, Mary 46, 47-50, 147
Stott, Robert and Annie 5
Surrender of Japanese 128, 135, 140

Tantalus 82, 83
Tapper, Bob 61, 151

Ukong 106, 128, 131, 137, 140, 160
Urlich, Dan 118

Wellun 40, 41
Westley, Jeff 158, 162, 163
Wigzell, Sgt Frank: ix; enlistment 92; first meeting with Stott 94; joining SOE 94; commando training 95-96; parachute training 97; insertion into Borneo 98-101; first operations in Borneo 105-7; introduction to headhunting 107; first encounters with Japanese 108; other operations 110-40; return to New Zealand 145; later life 147; correspondence with 158, 160, 162
Wilkinson, Sir Peter 43
Wingate, Pat 28, 29
Woodhouse, Colonel Chris viii-ix, 3, 35, 39, 43, 44, 147

Young, Horace 5, 72, 73, 75, 76

Zervas, Napoleon 3, 22